PRIMARY TO SECONDARY
Overcoming the Muddle in the Middle

Ruth Sutton
with illustration by Jim Whittaker

Published by Ruth Sutton Publications
St James's House
Pendleton Way
Salford M6 5FW
Tel No. +44(0)161 745 7444
Fax No. +44 (0)161 745 8999

Printed in Great Britain 2000
Reprinted in Great Britain 2001

Printed and bound in Great Britain by
Trinity Press, Salford, Greater Manchester

Acknowledgements

I am indebted to the hundreds of teachers who have shared their experience with me over the past decade and more. In particular, I would like to thank the Principals and staffs of the eleven schools in New Zealand with whom I worked on issues of student transition over the past eighteen months. Their patience and commitment, despite many other pressures on their time and energy, are greatly appreciated.   Thanks are also due to Diane Crew and her colleagues at the New Zealand Ministry of Education in Wellington for all their help and support.

As ever, the production of this book would not have happened without the continuing efforts of Mary McSherry, my right–hand person and painstaking DTP expert.   Nor would the book be complete without the off–the–wall vision and drawing skills of Jim Whittaker, our cartoonist.   My thanks to them both.

Contents

Introduction

Students' movement from one school to the next, and the impact on their learning, has been on my mind for many years. For a while I was Head of Lower School (Years 7–9) in an inner–city secondary school. I visited all the local primary schools, saw children and teachers at work there, talked to them about their hopes and anxieties around the move to the 'big school'. Despite all our efforts some of the incoming students really struggled with the simultaneous changes they faced, and we constantly reviewed and amended our systems and structures to meet their needs as much as we could.

For close to twenty years now I have been working with teachers and schools from all phases of the education service, firstly in England and then further afield. This has allowed me to focus on underlying issues as well as the more obvious steps we take, or not, to ease students through into the new environment and sustain the pace and quality of their learning. When the Ministry of Education in New Zealand offered me an opportunity to manage a special project on learning progression in the middle years, I was able to learn more, and finally inspired to write some of it down.

Perhaps inevitably, the issues have grown in complexity the longer I've looked at them. The simple solutions I would once have advocated have floundered often enough for me to recognise the assumptions which can shape our actions. I thought I knew most of what there was in teachers' minds about transition to secondary school before I set out to interview a few dozen of them, in depth and individually, as part of the New Zealand project. It was an illuminating experience. In the course of these interviews in October 1999, incidentally, I captured an earthquake on tape. It doesn't amount to a great deal as earthquakes go, just a rattling sound, then another, punctuated by the teacher and I giggling about whether we could both fit under the table.

The chapters follow a reasonably sequential pattern. In the first, I try to focus on the most important people, the children in our schools and their teachers. The four characters introduced here are composites, their views synthesised from countless conversations and experiences over the years. You should be able to recognise them as real people.

The second chapter looks through the other end of the telescope, to see the larger forces at work in our schools, and to review the conclusions of the most recent and interesting research into issues of learning and transition. From some of this research I draw the image of five bridges to be built between schools, to sustain the continuity of students' learning. Chapters three and four present the collective views of first students and then teachers, gathered in New Zealand over the past two years, and consider the implications of what they are saying.

In chapters five and six we return to the 'five bridges' and use the distinctions between them to categorise the practical strategies which schools can and do use to improve students' progression.

Each of Jim Whittaker's cartoons addresses an issue in the text close to where it is placed. Jim and I come from the same community, and taught in the same school for a while, where he still teaches Art. Each picture speaks volumes and is worth our attention in its own right, however discomforting the message may be.

There are fewer diagrams and visual images than in some of my other books perhaps because the complexity and interaction of different sides of the issue are hard to represent accurately in a visual image. I do have one to offer, however, which is quite minimal but sums up some of the vital relationship between teachers' attitudes, their communication with each other, and their use of the information they receive. Almost all that is written in the following pages relates to these factors and the connection between them.

FOUNDATIONS FOR LEARNING PROGRESSION

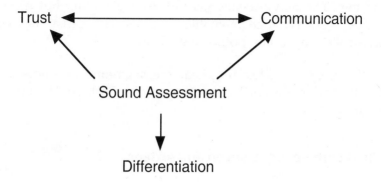

Chapter One:
Learning and Teaching Through the Ages

This Chapter heading sounds like the winner of the 'pompous title of the year' competition. It refers not to the history of learning and teaching but to the styles of learning and teaching that learners experience as they move through the school system. These styles change as the learner gets older, but in what ways? Is such change inevitable? Does it occur in easy stages or in big steps at certain points in the learner's life?

Let's look first at learning near the beginning of schooling - remembering always that learning is at its most rapid before the child starts school.

The Learners, aged seven and sixteen

The Seven-Year Old at School

Sara is seven. She stays in the same classroom for most of the day, except when she might be outside in the playground, or on an excursion beyond the school. She has worked with the same teacher for all her time at school this year. Two years ago, when she first started school Sara's teacher observed her really closely to find out as much as she could about Sara's experience to date, her skills and interests, the way she communicates and approaches different situations. The teacher also talked to Sara's parents about the things she did and said at home, what she enjoyed, what made her laugh, and about her pre-school activities. This teacher's observations and suggestions were passed on to the next teacher with care, both in writing and in conversation, and then from that teacher on to Sara's teacher in Year 2.

During the day Sara and her classmates work on a variety of activities, organised by the teacher. These activities are based on what the teacher knows about Sara's starting point and needs, and are also influenced by the learning expectations expressed in the National Curriculum. These curriculum guidelines are contained in big books which Sara has seen on the teacher's shelf. Every day they do some number work, and some reading and writing, but there are no bells to signify different periods of time. Sometimes they carry on doing something interesting beyond the time when they usually move on, and then the teacher rearranges things a little to pick up the activities they may have missed.

The teacher calls different parts of their learning by different names and most of the children understand what 'Science' is, but many of the things they learn about just merge together. Sara remembers a teacher coming from the next school and asking them about Social Studies, but none of the children were very clear what that meant.

Sometimes the teacher talks or reads to the whole class. Sometimes the children will work in groups together, based on friendship, or on the teacher's choice. Sometimes the children work individually on something, and the teacher will work alongside each child for a few minutes at a time, to check how learning is going, to make a decision about the next step for the child. Sara enjoys these talks with her teacher. They talk about what she's good at, what she's finding hard, and what she has to make a special effort with for the next few days or weeks.

Because she spends all her time with the same group of children, the teacher knows them really well, and they know her. Sara likes her present teacher a lot, but she wasn't so happy about the teacher she had last year, and was quite pleased when she moved on. This teacher seems to notice things really quickly, and can often prevent a child from being naughty or confused by intervening at the right time. Because they are together all the time, the teacher and the children develop routines for managing the classroom and the activities. Most of the children learn these routines quickly and Sara enjoys the sense of order and security which they provide. They help the teacher too, as daily tasks can be achieved quickly and effectively. Visitors to the classroom are often impressed by these routines, which seem to work so well.

The strong bond between the teacher and the children includes most of the parents too. The teacher will see many of them as they bring the children to school and wait at the end of the day to take them home. Sara's mother often has a word with the teacher on the days when she picks Sara up from school, and she can call her before schools starts in the morning if she's concerned about something. Like most of the other children, Sara lives within walking distance of her school.

Sara's teacher talked to the children at the start of the year about the importance of working together and supporting each other. She told them how geese fly in a V shape to protect each other and make the best progress. If one of the geese gets ill or tired and falls behind the rest, other geese will detach from the V to surround and support it. "That's the way I like us to work," said the teacher. "I'll support you, and you will support each other."

Apart from the reading, writing and Maths work they do every day, Sara's class do lots of other activities too. They make things to take home or to display around the room, which is full of colour and drawings and samples of the children's work. Sara has her own desk where she can keep her things, and her own place to hang her coat, with her name on it.

Sara doesn't get grades or scores on her work. Her teacher writes comments about what she's done well and what she needs to do next. Last year's teacher gave scores out of ten, and handed out lots of stickers, but this year's teacher doesn't do that. She said once that she would only give out 'Fantastic!' stickers for work which was really special, and she expects her children to do good work every day because they want to, not just to get a sticker.

On the children's report at the end of the year, the teacher will give Sara a number in some areas of her work, to give her mother an idea of how Sara is doing compared with other children of the same age. This happened last year too. Neither Sara or her mother are certain what these numbers actually mean, but the teacher said they showed that Sara was doing fine, on the whole.

That's a brief picture of Sara's experience of school, aged seven. Let's jump ahead a few years, into the secondary school in the same community, to see what learning is like for Tom.

The Sixteen Year Old at School

Tom, our sixteen year old student, is taught by eight teachers each week, in 50 minute spells. He and his friends move from classroom to classroom between lessons, sometimes having to walk from one end of the building to the other, or even to a neighbouring building. Bells signal the end of each spell and the start of the next. There are no secure lockers in the building, so students carry their books with them.

Each of Tom's teachers encounters between one hundred and two hundred students every week. It takes some of the teachers quite a while to learn the names of all their students, and even longer to understand the learning needs and capabilities of them all. Sometimes a teacher will teach a group for two years, but more often the students will go to a different teacher each year. Tom is not always sure that the teachers talk to each other much about their students, even within the same department, although there are bound to be some difficult students whom everyone talks about, and all the teachers seem to know one of Tom's friends who is very clever, and another boy who is a great soccer player.

Tom can remember his first year in this secondary school, when he wondered whether his teachers knew about what he had done in his previous school. Sometimes it felt as if they were starting all over again, although some of his teachers clearly were interested in what he had learned before and tried to build on that.

The week at school is broken up into teaching spells, with different subjects taught by different teachers. Tom has Maths every day, but he sees some of his other teachers only one or two days a week. Each time, they have to spend a few minutes reminding each other where they were 'up to' the last time they met. At the beginning of the year everyone is interested to see the 'timetable' which will determine the shape and feel of the week. Some days are definitely better than others. Some students talk among themselves about which afternoons they might be tempted to go downtown, when nothing on offer at school really appeals to them, or when they suspect the teachers might be slow to notice their absence. Other days become the highlight of the week, with just the right combination of activities. It's a bit of a lottery really.

When Tom first started at secondary school he enjoyed the variety of different lessons, with different people and different spaces, although it was a bit overwhelming, and tiring, for a while. Every now and then, though, it struck him that the things they were learning in different lessons were connected with each other, although no-one pointed out the connection. He had said something to one of his teachers about having learned something similar in another class and she'd replied, "Well, this time you're doing it properly", so he hadn't mentioned it again. Maybe things in Maths are completely different than in Technology or Social Studies, he thought to himself, and left it at that.

Now that he is in Year 11, they do work in groups occasionally in some of the classes, and he enjoys that. In earlier years, especially in some subjects, they did hardly any group work. One or two of the teachers had tried to make it work, but it didn't seem to happen as smoothly as it had in the primary school. Each teacher had different ways of organising things, and different ground-rules, and it was hard to remember who wanted what. Some of the students thought group work was babyish, although they didn't seem to mind it now. In their careers programme a number of the speakers had talked about the importance of working with others, group problem–solving and so on, and group work seemed to be back in again now.

Group work isn't the only difficult thing to organise when you see so many teachers. No–one seems clear about the routines in the class. Some teachers want the students to line up outside and wait for them at the start of a lesson. Others expect the students to be seated and getting on with something useful by the time the teacher reaches the room. Even the way they want work presenting varies from subject to subject. When Tom first started at the school, each subject teacher had marked and graded work in a different way, some using scores out of ten, others using letter grades, and the Art and English teachers didn't use grades or scores at all. That was OK, but it was hard to know how you were getting on in the different subjects. More recently the school had tried to make all the marking the same, but even so there seemed to be several different interpretations of the same codes. Now all the teachers used A–E letter grades for achievement, and 1–5 for effort, but Tom's Geography teacher had already told the group that he didn't want to use an A because, as he said, 'Nobody's perfect'. Tom made a mental note to avoid that teacher in next year's options if he could.

Tom's teachers are a mixed bunch. Some of them he hardly knows at all, and they hardly know him. One of them regularly calls him by his older brother's name. Other teachers, especially those he'd had for more than one year, Tom does feel close to, and would talk to if he needed to do so. When he first started at the school, he missed the relationship he'd had with his teacher in his last year at primary school, but as one of his friends had pointed out, it's fine to have one teacher most of the time if they're really good, but at least at secondary school you don't get stuck all week with someone you don't like, or who doesn't like you.

Tom's mother still gets confused about who teaches what and who she needs to see about various things. At least Tom's form tutor has stayed with the group since they started at the school, and his mother feels at ease and confident with him now, but at parents' evening she has to see all Tom's other teachers, or at least try to do so. One year his mother came home from parents' evening fairly certain that one of Tom's teachers had talked to her for five minutes about someone other than Tom, but she hadn't said anything about it at the time. She often says how different they all are, and what different impressions they give her of the same boy, her son.

As the exams have loomed over the students in the past year or two, the pace of teaching has really hotted up. Some of the students have asked one of their teachers to slow down as they weren't sure about some of the new material he was giving them, but he said he couldn't because they had to 'get through the syllabus' by the end of term, and they would just have to keep up.

Some of Tom's friends' parents have sent them for extra tuition in the evenings, but Tom's family couldn't afford it.

The other striking thing in the past few years has been how their grades have begun to reflect the grades in the external exams they are preparing for. That makes sense, so they can see how they might do in the exams, but it was pretty depressing to start with, when they were being compared with the expected achievement in an exam which was still over a year away. Their teachers have explained how in these exams they are being compared with students of their age all over the country, not just in their class or even their school, and they'd better get used to it. 'Someone has to fail, for the others to pass', was how one of the teachers explained it, but Tom wasn't very encouraged by that, as he wasn't clear what you had to do to pass, except be better than someone else.

Tom is a good student. He enjoys school. He likes the variety of both teachers and subjects, and the wide range of things to do after school, the big band he plays with, and access to the computer room at lunchtime. He loves to see his friends every day. But he doesn't feel that anyone really understands him personally as a learner, except perhaps his tutor, who doesn't teach him at all this year. He wishes there was more chance to connect the various things he was being taught. He wants a clearer idea of how he is getting on, and what he needs to do to get better grades.

The Teachers, in the Primary and the Secondary School

Sahida Chaudhry is an excellent teacher. She works in the primary school where Sara is a student. Sahida did her B.Ed several years ago. She wanted to be a teacher from quite an early age, but wasn't sure until much later whether to teach younger or older students. She could have gone to University to read Maths, and then on into teaching, but she decided in the end that the primary years were more important and that's where she wanted to teach. Her parents weren't happy about it – they felt she was wasting her talents – but they didn't stand in her way. Some of Sahida's friends teach in the secondary sector. They don't understand either why she would want to spend her days with young children who need 'looking after', rather than 'teaching'. They do argue occasionally about what teaching actually is. She says her job is to introduce the child to the world, whereas their job is to introduce the world to the child, and the two activities start with different assumptions and involve different priorities.

Sahida likes and appreciates the flexibility and choices her primary teaching job gives her. Her days are not dictated by bells and timetables, except the one she creates for herself to ensure that the week's activities are reasonably balanced. In the past few years, the National Curriculum has had more influence on what she teaches, but how she does it is still largely up to her, using her experience and what she knows about the learning habits and needs of her children. The number of children in her class went up recently to the point where this attention to needs was more difficult, but this year the numbers are better.

So, her teaching plans specify the things she wants her children to learn from any given activity. The expected outcomes may be different for different groups of children in her class, and different again for the two children who have special statements of learning need. She arranges the working groups depending on the type of activity, and the purpose of the group in each case. She tries to vary the types of teaching, and the introduction of the 'Literacy Hour' has made her focus more on whole class teaching and questioning.

When the National Curriculum was first introduced, all the teachers worried about the need to 'cover' everything, but now – several years on – they've realised that even if you teach everything the children won't necessarily learn everything, and the focus on learning has re-asserted itself in the school. 'Teach less better' was their unofficial school slogan last year, unofficial because they weren't sure how the school inspectors might react if they knew that the teachers had agreed which bits of some of the Curriculum documents were 'expendable' for some children.

Sahida knows it's worth spending quite a while at the beginning of each year establishing the climate and the routines she wants in her classroom. These may not be the same as in other rooms in the school, but the children have a year to benefit from them, and she finds that taking time over this really pays dividends in the end.

Another thing she makes a real effort with is the display in her room, to make it as stimulating and colourful as she can. She remembers how bare some of the classrooms were when she was at secondary school, although others were amazingly different, full of pictures and students' work. In her English teacher's room she still remembers the poems written on the ceiling! And the Maths rooms had shapes and models hanging from the ceiling, which was one of the things she loved about Maths.

Sahida believes that the social habits and skills of the classroom are just as important as the more academic aspects of what she offers her students. She thinks about how children learn, and the circumstances most likely to encourage learning, and that's what she tries to establish in her room. She's interested in Maths, and loves teaching it, but she knows that Maths doesn't stand alone, unconnected to other things she presents to her students.

She teaches the oldest children in the school, in the year before they transfer to secondary school. She remembers what a big step this was in her learning life, and tries to explain to her children, especially towards the end of the year, what may face them in the secondary school. She still remembers her time in secondary school very clearly. She offers her children the best advice she can think of, to help them understand what a big step it is into secondary school. "The road to learning is full of potholes to start with," she explains to her children. "Next year, the teachers will want you to be running on a smooth learning road, with all the potholes filled in. This is our last chance to fill in your potholes, because next year the teachers will be too busy to help you like I can. Most important, you have to learn to help yourself, because you'll have to work more on your own in the secondary school, and not in groups like you do here."

Sahida hasn't been in a secondary classroom since she was at school herself, but she doesn't think it's changed much since she was there. She wants to encourage her children to treat the move to the next school very seriously. For those who are confident of their ability to take the change in their stride, her advice is fine. For other children who lack this confidence, Sahida doesn't realise that she's reinforcing their anxiety about secondary school, and their fear that they may not do well there. All the children are hearing about secondary school from other sources too, from their older siblings and from older children in the community, some of whom think it's funny to warn them about being bullied, or getting lost. The combined impact of all this on less confident children is to undermine their perseverance later: when they encounter difficulties as many children do during the first weeks and months in the new school, they see this as a fulfilment of their fears, and lose heart.

Sahida is proud of her role as a primary school teacher. Like many other educators over the past decade or so, this pride has been threatened or even undermined by repeated criticism of teachers from politicians and others. She has felt defensive, knowing that her teaching could always be better, but that she doesn't deserve the blame for the alleged declining academic standards of the nation's young people. "I do a good job" she says, "but I can't be responsible for what happens to these children when they leave me and move on. Maybe the teachers in the next school need to examine the effectiveness of what they do. Some of my children come back and see me from time to time when they've started at the next school. Some of them tell me they're repeating things we did here. Others feel lost, and that no-one really cares about them." She hesitates. "Secondary school teachers seem to look down on us, because they're specialists in a subject. Well, I'm a specialist too. I specialise in children's learning. I know that sounds a bit righteous, but I'm fed up with being patronised at best and blamed at worst."

Ben Smith is an excellent teacher. He has been teaching for about as long as Sahida. He did an English degree, then went into advertising for a while before realising that he really wanted to teach. Now he's Deputy Head of an English department in a large secondary school, teaching four senior exam groups and one younger class. He teaches some of the children who were in Sahida's class last year, but he has never met her.

Ben was drawn into teaching by his passion for literature, which began while he was at school himself, continued through university, lay dormant for a while and then became irresistible. He doesn't expect to become a published writer himself, and instead he wants to encourage young people to share his passion. It was always adolescents he wanted to teach, and only English.

As a joke once, when the department was faced with describing its 'aims and objectives' in yet another school self-review exercise, Ben suggested that they just write on the complicated plan 'Our aim is to unlock the treasure house of literature' and send it back to the Principal.

When he sits back and thinks about it, the way teaching is organised in the school doesn't make a lot of sense to him, although he rarely sits back and thinks about it. For as long as he can remember, that's the way teaching has worked in every secondary school he's known. You have a room (if you're lucky), the students come to you, you develop something special between you for an hour or less and then they go away again, and another group arrives. The room is definitely his, not theirs. The students don't really have a place they can call their own until they get older and can use the senior common room. Last year, for some timetabling reason he was never sure about, Ben didn't teach in the same room all the time. He didn't like that at all, and was pleased when he got his old room back this year. One of his colleagues has taught in the same room for as long as he's been on the staff – twenty three years!

During the teaching spells Ben focusses entirely on his students, and he assumes and expects that they will focus entirely on him and their shared work. Ben is not particularly interested in what they do elsewhere with other people. English is his passion. He does his best to make it so for as many students as possible. Part of his mission, as he calls it, is to teach his students how to write, in all sorts of forms and styles. He's aware that the History department are also teaching essay writing skills, and he's not happy about some of what they're doing but it's hard to find time to talk to them about it. Since the school went to a split lunchtime to get all the students through the cafeteria, there's no time when all the teachers are together for more than a few minutes, except for after school meetings and professional development days, most of which are quite tightly programmed and don't allow for teachers to talk to each other about day-to-day things.

Of all his teaching, Ben enjoys most the time he spends with the older students, who have chosen English as a major option, and with whom he can be more himself. Some of them clearly share his enthusiasm, and combine it with the energy of their adolescence. Each year he revels in the small number of students who are aiming to study English at University. For them, contact with him as their teacher is a life-changing experience.

To some extent, teaching the younger students is for Ben a necessary price to pay for the joy of teaching the older ones. They are different people altogether, needing different things from him which he does his best to offer but isn't sure he's very good at it. He enjoys them, but doesn't spend a lot of time preparing for them, relying on performance rather than planning to hold their attention. He knows this might not be as effective as it could be for all the younger students. He feels constrained by time, and the impossibility – in his own mind – of treating each of them as individuals, in the way he does with his seniors. Every week he sees 100 students. He cannot plan for each of them individually, or provide for the enormous range of learning needs. One of his colleagues refers to his younger students as 'munchkins', which is affectionate but doesn't perceive them as serious learners.

Ben has certain assumptions about the starting points of his young students. He expects them to be able to read – for meaning, not just recognising the words. He also expects that they will be able to express themselves in writing with reasonable accuracy. If reading and writing are not confident and capable, he isn't always sure how best to help. The Special Needs team in the school are very effective in dealing with children with the most severe difficulties, and over the years he has learned a great deal from them about modifying written resources to make them more accessible to less confident readers, but sometimes he resents having to do so. This has little to do with what he perceives as his core purpose, which is **literature not literacy.**

He does occasionally use groups for teaching, and he always has his room arranged with the desks in small groups, or in a circle. Moving the desks and chairs into rows is a form of temporary punishment, until the students show that they can work together sensibly. Ben doesn't often see areas of the school other than the block he teaches in, but on the occasional forays elsewhere to do a cover lesson or to find someone, he's aware that some teachers have the students in rows facing the front all the time. The students in his tutor group talk to him sometimes about the different expectations, methods and rules which they experience with different teachers, and how confusing it can be.

Ben has always had a tutor group in the senior school. He really enjoys his time with them, brief though it may be. He prides himself on the quality of these relationships, and if he actually teaches any of his own tutor group the bond with those students can get very strong. But that's an accident of the timetable. The person who does the timetable always says that it's the part–time teachers' classes which have to be organised first, then the senior classes, then the junior classes, and anything lower down the priority list than that probably won't happen. To Ben, the school timetable seems to be one of those uncontrollable factors which has a great influence on his teaching life.

For the youngest students in the school, Ben is aware of the information which has been gathered about their prior learning, their skills and needs, as they transfer into the new school. He believes strongly that the students should be able to make a 'fresh start' in terms of their behaviour and relationships, so he doesn't want to look at all the past records, even if he had time to do so. On the learning side, Ben knows it would be useful to know beforehand about the patterns and trends of prior achievement among the students, so that he could adjust his plans. But as we have seen, he tends to rely on inspiration rather than detailed planning, and is outfaced by the detail in the records which he feels he has no chance to really take account of. He relies instead on the first few weeks of the new school year to provide him with information about his students, and trusts that the real talent will reveal itself in the end.

The schemes of work for the younger students are designed by the teachers themselves, although they too—like their primary colleagues — have to take account of the prescribed expectations in the National Curriculum. For the older students, the over-riding need is to cover the exam syllabus or prescription. When Ben joined the department, there were no schemes of work for the exam classes, just the exam regulations and the list of texts to be covered, but things have improved since then. Ben is experienced and confident enough now to be selective about what he deals with in depth and detail and what he just skims, but his less experienced colleagues seem very anxious to cover everything, and end up teaching too much too fast for some of their students. "Teach less, better" is Ben's private motto, but his Head of Department is unsure about it. "What happens if there's a big question on the exam on something we haven't covered? Parents will be complaining straight away." Ben's reply is always the same, "We can cover it, but if the students don't learn it they still can't do the question on the exam and we've not gained anything. We have to motivate first, and you don't do that by covering too much too fast." The argument remains unresolved.

For their first year students, Year 7, the English team have tended to plan from an assumption that children will have covered, and learned, all the aspects of language specified in the National Curriculum for the pre-secondary age range. The only exceptions will be those children who have a special statement of learning need, for whom special programmes are planned and responsibility shared with the Special Needs people. Among the incoming group of students, there will be a few to look out for, usually concerning behaviour, and sometimes children who are especially talented in some way. The children entering Ben's school come from thirty or more primary schools, although over half come from the three closest ones. Despite the National Curriculum which applies to all of them, it's the skill and talent of individual teachers which seems to have most impact on the starting point of the children, and there's not much the English team can do about that. They know that it's not really effective to treat most of the new students as if they're working at the same level, but that's still basically what happens. Gradually, working as a team, they are sharing resources and developing activities to engage children at different levels, but it will take a while to do this for all the modules in Year 7.

In recent years, the records which have accompanied the incoming children have allocated a 'level' to various aspects of their achievement. These levels are ostensibly based on the descriptions in the National Curriculum guidelines, but to Ben and his colleagues these numbers signify very little. Sometimes the level seems to bear no relationship to the ability demonstrated by the child in their first 'diagnostic' activities at the start of term. The English department themselves aren't as clear about these 'levels' as they are about the exam grades they apply to the higher years, based on years of 'moderating', discussion and exemplars.

Recently, another use has been found for these levels, as the baseline for the 'value-added' data which the school now insists on gathering, but the English department are not convinced about that exercise, and prefer to set their own tests to ascertain the students' 'baseline'. This usually reveals performance lower than that claimed by the previous teachers, which undermines even more the credibility of the 'transfer information'. The secondary teachers believe that their information is more realistic and allows for more accurate measurement of true value-added over the following few years.

The 'value-added' focus is just a symptom of the change which has taken place in the education service in the past several years, some of which Ben is very sceptical about. He feels under pressure from the pace of curriculum and other changes, and defensive about vague but high-profile claims that the quality of teaching and student achievement is not as high as it should be. He feels strongly that he and his colleagues do the best job they can with the children they get. He has not been trained to teach children how to read, and doesn't really think it's part of his job. If children arrive in secondary school unable or unwilling to learn what he wants and needs to teach them, then it must be necessary to review what's happening to them earlier.

The Muddle in the Middle

Sara and Tom, Sahida and Ben are not real people: they merely represent learners and teachers in two stages of the education service. They are presented here not to represent right or wrong, but merely differences.

At the two extremes of the age range of compulsory education learning and teaching reflect different goals and purposes. In the early years, teachers are clear and confident about their aim to introduce the learner to the world. The child is at the centre, and learning is designed to be as holistic and flexible as the child herself. For the sixteen year-old, learning is divided into 'subjects', and teaching is fragmented too, with specialist 'subject' teaching teams. Their goal is to introduce the world to the student through the vehicle of their specialist knowledge. Such knowledge is highly valued at this stage, and the holistic approach to learning has by now been largely set aside.

One could discuss *ad infinitum* (if not *ad nauseam*) the various merits of these respective perceptions of knowledge, 'subjects' and teaching, but the fact is that they both exist, and in many education systems they are the hallmark of the change in learning and teaching as the child grows older. The question here is how and when the change from one to the other of these approaches should be managed. What is the impact of this change on the structures of schooling, on the training and work of teachers, and on the successful learning and progress of the students themselves?

If both ends of the age range are clear about what they are doing, it appears that somewhere between the two we are faced with a 'muddle in the middle'. During the middle years of schooling, for children aged between around nine or ten and thirteen or fourteen, we do not appear to know how best to provide for them. They may be old enough to cope successfully with more than one teacher, but not comfortable with eight or more. They may be ready to leave the relative cosiness of the primary classroom, but not yet ready to be dropped unaided into the 'big school' and to face the 'big kids' who inhabit it.

Having looked briefly at the experiences of the most important people in the education service, the students and their teachers, let's focus for a while on the structures and systems which surround their work, and on what educational research is also telling us about the continuity of children's learning. As we do so, the 'chicken and egg' question will be, 'Is it the structures of schooling which have determined different ways of learning and teaching in primary and secondary schools, or have the structures themselves been based on different approaches to learning and teaching?'

One big question

What would you suggest, to enable Shahida and Ben to understand each other better?

Chapter Two:
Structures, Systems and Research

The experiences of the students and teachers recounted in Chapter One would be recognisable in many education systems round the world. Each of the people described in the chapter works within an institution which has certain structures, both of space and time, and is bound by certain systems, many of which arise from the structures they have to serve. Sometimes it's hard to distinguish the assumptions on which the structures are based, but here are a few for a start.

Some Starting Assumptions

1. Young children can't be expected to travel far to school, so primary schools will be relatively small and situated in the middle of residential communities. In inner urban areas, where the population is particularly concentrated, these schools may be larger, but they will be within walking distance for most of their children.

2. The learning needs of young children focus particularly around learning to read and write, to handle number, to work with others, to develop physical and creative growth and curiosity. These basic skills, and others, can then be harnessed to learn more knowledge and skills, and the ability to apply them. As the basic skills connect so closely with each other, and with the child's overall development, it makes sense for them to be managed by a single teacher, working in a single multi-purpose space.

3. The design of primary schools follows from these starting points, with spaces occupied by teachers who each have particular responsibility for a group of learners. There may be walls between these spaces, or teachers may share a larger space, but the focus of teaching is usually on the individual child, with whom an individual teacher forms a close bond for a year or more.

4. As children grow, they become more aware of themselves as part of a wider world. Since the European Renaissance, this wider world has tended to differentiate human knowledge into 'specialisms', and to value the acquisition and demonstration of specialist knowledge. Over the past few centuries, the trend towards specialisation has accelerated, with consequences for the structures of education.

5. One of the functions of secondary schooling, to justify its cost, has been the identification and selection of those young people who will maintain and develop the structures of the society in which they live. The learning needs of this 'elite' will be met by institutions of 'higher education', and the schools are asked to prepare some students at least for such a path, which will include introduction to 'specialist' knowledge, skills and understanding.

6. Another ascribed role for secondary schools is the preparation of larger numbers of young people for the work place, who may need a modicum of training to make them more 'employable.' To the degree that the world of work has changed and continues to do so, the characteristics of 'employability' also change, causing further shifts in the goals and strategies of secondary schooling, which in turn affect the structures of the school and the priorities of those who work in them.

There are other assumptions, of course. One which must be mentioned, although it will not be examined in detail here, is that an effective democracy demands a publicly–funded high–quality education service for all its children, not just those being groomed for future stardom.

The Muddle in the Middle

There seems to be, in my mind at least, some certainty about the purpose and strategies for teaching at both ends of the age spectrum – in the early years and the final stages of institutionalised learning. But the question remains: at what age and stage does the learner shift from one structure to the next? Is there a 'muddle in the middle' and what's to be done about it?

The pursuit of effective learning outcomes – if this were the only criterion – would dictate that a learner would move from one 'structure' to the next when he or she was ready to do so, and that there would be no fixed chronological steps to be followed. In reality, the pursuit of effective learning outcomes is not the only criterion for the design of our structures: in a political process dominated by choices about taxation, the other key criterion is cost, and it is issues of cost which dominate decisions about structures, no matter what rhetoric may be presented to the contrary.

A huge variety currently exists in the school structures catering for students aged between 9 and 14. There are middle schools, usually covering three or four year cohorts of students, although in New Zealand the Intermediate schools cater for just two years, aged 11–13. There are all through schools, usually in isolated rural areas, and these were quite common in some parts of the UK until the 1950s. There are 'junior high' schools (aged 10 or 11 to 14), and senior high schools. There are 11–18 high schools, and 11–16 high schools, with some 'sixth form college' or 'junior college' after that. In some local school systems in England, usually for historical reasons and local government reorganisations, different school structures may exist side by side, although gradually the differences are being ironed out. The muddle in the middle is clearly reflected in structures: a more important concern is whether the muddle also exists in approach to teaching and learning.

Decisions about structures, which in many systems were taken many decades ago on the basis of the assumptions of the age, materialise literally into buildings, which then form the basic infrastructure, expensive both to provide and to change. In addition, the physical structures of education create human structures, training patterns and career paths for example, which inspire loyalty based as much on self–interest as on any theory of learning or educational principles. The differing purposes of primary and secondary education, their physical size and layout, also create different organisational climates which affect the attitudes and behaviour of those who work there. Certain ways of working come to appear 'natural' and others 'unnatural': seeing things from a different perspective becomes more difficult and therefore more rare.

In their approach to change, educators often feel inhibited about acknowledging self–interest as a legitimate motivation in a profession ostensibly devoted to the promotion of the interests of the students and their families. But the quality of that service depends essentially upon the motivation and skills of the educators: it would be folly to ignore the motivation of the teachers in some high–minded pursuit of the motivation of the learners. If the self–interest of educators is a barrier to change which could be in the interests of improved learning, then we must be interested in 'what's in it for the teachers' or the enterprise will fail. A further barrier to reasoned reflection, even before change can be contemplated, is a culture of blame.

A Culture of Blame

Any effective examination of differences between primary and secondary education and 'the muddle in the middle' needs to be approached without blame. Sometimes blame is directed towards educators as a whole, for their inflexibility or other apparent inadequacies. More commonly, blame is directed from one set of educators towards fellow teachers on the 'other side' of the education service. Blame grows when we ourselves feel under attack. It's a form of protection against guilt or responsibility for something which is not going well. If we all felt that all our children were learning and progressing as well as is possible, there would be no need for blame. But the past decade has undermined much of our professional confidence and pride. Educators in many countries and systems have been systematically criticised and blamed for a host of things, from

declining standards of spelling to the rise in teenage drug abuse. The public have been encouraged to lose faith in teachers, and even if parents have been slow to do so, the indirect impact has been that many teachers and schools have lost faith in themselves.

If we start from the loud (though unproven) assumption that real standards of achievement are falling – for students and by implication for their teachers too – then blame will not be far behind. The thoughts of the two teachers presented in Chapter One about the work of teachers in other stages of the service have been expressed to me repeatedly by teachers in both informal conversation and formal interviews. Questioning the effectiveness of others is a perfectly understandable reaction from people who are being collectively accused of incompetence. The problem, however, is that such blame requires others to act rather than ourselves. It can exacerbate that very feeling of being hopeless and helpless which undermines teachers' own self–efficacy while they are charged with increasing the self–efficiacy of their students.

There are further reasons too why schools in different phases have been less trusting of each other in the past several years. Judgements of school quality are based more than ever before on the quantification of measurable outcomes, the comparison of these outcomes with schools in like circumstances, and the attempt to account for the 'value–added' by the school through comparing the students' performance on entry to their performance on exit. All these strategies are fraught with technical difficulties which are well–understood but seem to carry little weight compared with high–stake public reports on schools' 'performance'. If these public reports are used to influence parental choice of school, and thereby the numbers on roll, the school's budget and the number of teachers to be employed, the link between the presentation of schools' measured outcomes and teachers' job security is clear.

Schools face a strong temptation to react to these pressures in ways which exacerbate the tension between primary and secondary. Firstly, secondary schools can point to the poor achievement of their incoming students as a reason for their poor performance later. Secondly, teachers may underestimate this incoming performance as a way of improving the 'value–added' of the school. The interests of primary schools lie in demonstrating the strength of achievement prior to transfer, which has not been built upon later. The temptation to blame is strong and has to some extent been forced upon us: it takes courage and confidence to reject blame as an option and to look for more productive solutions.

Recognition of complexity

If a resolution of the 'muddle in the middle' problem was easy we would have cracked it by now. It is in fact fraught with complexity. First, it has to be established, as empirically as possible, that there is truly a muddle in the middle, and that this is damaging the learning and development of some of our students. Second, we need to accept the complexity of the problem, and that a single strategy is unlikely to 'fix' it. Third, if it is the case that the main components of the muddle are attitudinal rather than structural, then we face a harder task which could easily slip into the 'too hard' basket, and perseverance is required. Finally, the need to review the middle years of schooling can be seen as an opportunity to challenge some of our most fundamental assumptions about learning and teaching, not as a means of beating ourselves up, but as part of what all good learners do all the time – reflect, review and set goals for improvement.

> *Here's a story about school improvement, from Canada. The school in question was regarded by its teachers and its community as a good school. Involvement in a school improvement project was thought to be unnecessary by some of the staff. "If it ain't broke, don't fix it," they said. But the group charged with looking for a school–based improvement project decided to focus on a small of ninth graders who seemed to be at odds with the general climate*

of achievement. These students, a fraction of the grade level and a minute proportion of the school as a whole, were falling behind, on the verge of dropping out, dissatisfied and disruptive in many of their classes. When it was suggested that these students should be the target of a whole–school improvement project, there was strenuous argument against. Although it was recognised that the school was not succeeding with these students, it was felt that they represented too small a range of issues to be of interest to the rest of the school. There was also some resentment that in focussing on a small number of disaffected students, the achievements of the rest were being ignored.

Nevertheless, the project went ahead. The students' circumstances, learning and motivation, were all examined thoroughly. Their individual difficulties were revealed to the extent that they were seen as individuals rather than as a 'group' as they had been seen previously. All sorts of interesting information came to light, which had relevance for wider issues of learning and teaching in all grade levels not just Grade Nine. The outcomes of the project in terms of changes in both attitudes and practice went way beyond the original focus.

One of the researchers involved with the project reported a conversation with a more sceptical staff member. "It was as if we started looking at the school as a wall with tiny windows in it" the teacher had said. "From a distance, very little of the view beyond the wall could be seen through the tiny window we had chosen. But the closer we got to the window, the more of the view beyond it was revealed to us. Eventually, as we looked through the window, its small size was irrelevant, as what we saw beyond it was the total view. That project showed us things about our school that went way beyond the small group of ninth graders with problems. What we found were problems for us not just for them, and

*the spinoffs were much more wide–ranging than we would
ever have predicted."*

The 'muddle in the middle' of our education service, even if
affects only a small proportion of our students, is a window we
need to get close to, because of what it may show us about
learning and teaching as a whole, during the middle years, and
beyond. It is not about finding the best age for all children to
move from one form of schooling to the next. There never is one
right age for all children to do anything: readiness for change
depends on so many variables that it would be fruitless to seek
absolute conclusions about the chronology of transfer. What we
might seek, however, is information about what happens to
children in the transfer from primary–type to secondary–type
schooling, at whatever age this occurs. If this coincides with a
move from one school to another, from small school to large, or
from local school to one further away, what is the combined
impact of several changes at once. What impact does puberty
have? Does parental involvement change at transfer, and if so
why and how? Can recent educational research help us at all, to
identify the problem if not to suggest some solutions?

Recent Research Findings

The implementation of National testing and school inspection in
England and Wales over the past decade is producing a plethora
of statistical data about the measured learning outcomes of
students at different stages, and the apparent effectiveness of
schools' strategies across a wide range of issues. For a while the
emphasis was on outcomes of the early years of schooling, in
addition to the continuing interest in the outcomes of high–stake
assessments at 16+ and 18+. More recently, however, concern
has been generated about the stages in between, with students
aged between around 9–10 and 13–14. There had always been a
backdrop of largely anecdotal evidence about what happens to
learning and motivation when children move to 'the big school',
and now the evidence was accumulating to add depth and rigour

to the research. A further development has been the interest in the views of the children themselves, sometimes under–valued in the past as too subjective to be credible, and requiring too much time and patience to investigate.

From these two types of sources – assessment data and the results of student interviews – a research team from Homerton College, University of Cambridge, gathered the fullest picture to date in the United Kingdom of 'The Impact of School Transition and Transfer on Pupils' Attitudes to Learning and their Progress'. Significantly, the research was both commissioned and published by the Department for Education and Employment (Research Report RR 131, September 1999).

The authors, Maurice Galton, John Gray and Jean Rudduck, reviewed all the existing relevant research in the UK and North America, to which they themselves had also contributed over the years. They included a focus on year–to–year transitions as well as school– to– school transfers. In England and Wales, the usual age for student transfer from primary to secondary schooling is 11, but the research looked at this transition at whatever age it occurs. Their starting point was that "we need young people who can sustain, through primary and secondary schooling

- an enthusiasm for learning

- confidence in themselves as learners

- a sense of achievement and purpose."

The full text of their report deserves to be studied in detail. Some of the findings are pertinent to systems beyond the UK as well as within it: among these are the following points:

1. Only a small number of studies have focused on the impact of transfer on academic progress, while many more have looked at the personal and social effects.

2. Even after allowance is made for the 'summer dip' (ie the effect on learning of the long school holiday, often six to eight weeks or even more), it is clear that many students experience a 'hiatus' in learning after transfer. The authors estimate that "two out of five students fail to make progress during the year immediately following the change of schools."

3. Even when the curriculum is prescribed for both the 'providing' and 'receiving' schools to create a continuous learning programme between the two, variations in the interpretation and depth of treatment can lead to unexpected discontinuities, particularly in teaching methods rather than in content.

4. Some secondary teachers still cling to the principle of the 'fresh start'.

5. Policies of 'parental choice' have fragmented previous connections between schools and led to secondary schools dealing with a larger number of 'providing' schools. This is especially the case with single sex schools in large conurbations. One girls' secondary school in central Auckland, New Zealand, draws students from 75 pre–secondary schools, and this number would not be unusual in many other schools in major cities across the UK. It is certainly not conducive to a planned strategy for preparation and induction for each individual student. Even though the inadequacies of 'fresh start' are understood, it is a tempting solution to an otherwise tricky problem. In this as in other areas of education policy, central political decisions have exacerbated a problem, leaving schools to pick up the pieces through their newly–devolved responsibilities.

The phrase 'opening a can of worms' springs to mind at this point! There seems little doubt that a problem exists. Two out of five students failing to make expected progress in the year after transfer is too high a proportion to be shrugged off as 'natural wastage' or consigned to the 'too hard' basket. Similar statistics may not yet be available for students in Canada, or Australia, or New Zealand, or various states of the USA, but one wonders whether they would be very different.

The researchers did not confine themselves to looking at the assessment scores and performance of students before and after transfer. They were interested too in the students' attitude to school, and the level of 'engagement' in their work, measured both by observation and through interviews. From this it appeared that some students, although continuing to do well, were being 'turned off' school after the initial stimulus of transfer to the new school had worn off. This phenomenon was particularly noted in the two major American reviews of research, conducted by A. Wigfield et al. in 1991 and by E.M.Anderman and M.L.Maehr in 1994. (See the 'Further Reading' list for details). The Homerton study shows how the research evidence

1. highlights the significance of transfer for students' motivation and sense of 'self–as–learner';

2. offers evidence of a downturn in motivation following the initial period of adjustment;

3. emphasises the importance for students at this age of their school career of social interactions and affiliations; and

4. explains the downturn in terms of loss of self–esteem in a larger and more overtly competitive environment and of the mismatch between students' emerging sense of adulthood and the tendency for schools to regard the new intake as novices.

Unsurprisingly, the research indicates that students from the poorest homes and those with existing learning difficulties suffer most negative consequences from both the long summer break and from transfer to a new school, with language skills declining more markedly than Maths. More surprisingly, the subject/ learning area most vulnerable to the impact of transfer was found to be Science, where only 35% of students were observed to be 'engaged' after transfer, compared with over 60% previously.

From their examination of how schools are currently dealing with transfer issues, the authors of the study present five categories of response, which have been described as the 'Five Bridges' which schools can build across the 'gulf'. (Michael Barber, 'Bridges to Assist a Difficult Crossing', in the Times Educational Supplement, London, March 12th 1999.) I will explain these bridges here, and then return to them in the final Chapters of this book as a means of classifying the wide range of suggested ways forward which have been gathered from our experience in the UK and elsewhere.

The Five Bridges across the Primary to Secondary divide.....

The managerial/ bureaucratic bridge

These strategies involve the Headteachers/Principals of schools in a community keeping in regular touch with each other, to provide accurate information about each others' needs and expectations, and to present their practice to each other. This bridge is particularly useful in communities where the catchment areas of schools are reasonably clearly defined and the number of schools providing students for a local high school does not run to more than a dozen or so. In some cases, where the rolls of some of the schools are less than healthy, the purpose of better communication may be overwhelmed by the need to 'sell' the school to the wider community.

The social and personal bridge

These strategies involve helping the child to come to terms with the new environment of the 'big' school. Trips to the new school are organised, for a good look round and some degree of 'orientation', finding the key areas, locating toilets (always an anxiety for children), meeting some of the older students. These visits can take place before the students move across, and might involve taking part in some activities, use of specialist resources, or attending concerts, and so on. Visits can take place the other way too, with teachers and students from the secondary school spending time in neighbouring primary schools. A wide range of possible purposes and activities are suggested later.

The curriculum content bridge

National and provincial curriculums have been written and amended in recent years with the deliberate purpose of planning for continuity of learning as students move from one school to the next. The research seems to indicate that this exercise – merely writing and publishing teaching expectations – has had little impact on the actual continuity of learning. Differences of training, confidence, perspective and interpretation still have a marked influence on teachers' and schools' management of these programmes.

Families of school can use the prescribed curriculums as the starting point for some shared planning, assisted by the common language in the headings and nomenclature of the shared curriculum statements. Until and unless they get into the detail and start talking things through, and sharing examples of activities and expectations, the problem of discontinuity remains. When teachers expect to understand each other and then discover that they don't, the task of developing continuity seems even harder than before.

The pedagogical bridge

The three bridges mentioned so far are relatively easy to address, but seem to have little positive impact on their own. The last two are much more problematic, but do seem to make a difference. When the manageable things don't seem to work, and the things that might work are too hard, it's no surprise to find the issue remains a problem year after year.

Many years ago, David Hargreaves' study of teaching and learning in the Inner London Education Authority concluded that it was how children were taught rather than what they were taught that made the difference as they moved from school to school. The Homerton College team reach very similar conclusions, and my own recent study of eleven schools in and around Wellington, New Zealand supports this too. Primary and secondary school teachers do seem to teach differently: the interesting question is whether it is the approach to teaching which has generated different teaching structures, or the other way around.

In Chapter Four I present the voices and views of teachers talking about this issue, but one snapshot from those interviews provides an indication of the connection between school structures and teaching methods.

> *Mary is a skilled and experienced teacher in a New Zealand Intermediate school (a two year middle school for students in Years 7 and 8). The traditional pattern of teaching in this and many other Intermediate schools has been the primary model of one teacher with one class, although children at this stage go to different teachers in specialist areas for 'Technicraft'. Very recently, and after much debate, Mary's school moved into 'semi–specialisation' in which for half the day students visit different teachers for some specialist teaching, in teaching spells lasting about an hour.*

> *Mary was fascinated by the impact which this structural change was having on her teaching. "I see these children*

only for a few hours each week," she said, " and on only two or three occasions, so days can go by in between. We have to spend a few minutes each time I see them recalling what we did last time. I see so many more children each week now that I don't know their particular learning needs and find myself providing only one or two variations on the same task even though I know that some of the children will be struggling or bored. Just at the point where I've got them settled down and I've managed to get round everyone, it's time to pack up. I'll get used to it I suppose. Many of the teachers like it because it gives them a chance to focus on teaching what they enjoy and do well, and the children like the variety, but at the moment I'm finding it frustrating."

Mary is an exceptionally skilled classroom teacher, who began her career teaching younger children. Her expectations of herself and her children are very high. These include an intimate knowledge of the learning needs of each of her students, and the daily habit of developing activities tailored to those needs. She aims for a high level of 'on task' engagement of her students, which takes a while to achieve and then can be maintained for longer than an hour. The schedule of activities she is used to planning in her own classroom is more flexible than the schedule now operating in the school. Now the end of each teaching spell is marked with a siren sound which determines the children's movement from one teacher to the next.

It is not surprising that the classroom pedagogy of primary and secondary teachers is so different, given the enormous differences in the structures of time and space which dictate the organisation of teaching. (More of these differences and their implications will be explored in Chapter Six.) Even so, schools interested in crossing the pedagogical bridge without necessarily changing structures can focus on some shared teaching strategies which will be experienced by the children in the pre–secondary context and then be used again by their teachers in the new school, making a clear and planned link in 'ways of working' between the two. Ideally, the teachers will work together initially to learn the strategies and become aware of how they might be used in different contexts.

The strategies in question here may include collaborative group work, task planning skills, self–correction skills, review and goal–setting, and so on. Many of these are taught and used to great effect in pre–secondary classrooms, but then not used again for a while, or employ techniques which the students don't recognise. If these skills are assumed or re–taught in the new school, the connection with previous experience may not be made overtly for the students because the new teachers simply do not know how the previous classroom operated. One might expect that the students will make the connection themselves, and point it out to the new teachers, but there are a host of reasons why this very rarely happens.

Serious efforts to cross the pedagogical bridge were found in only one school in twenty in the Homerton study. Even more rare – in only one school in fifty – was evidence of a focus on the fifth of the five bridges.

The 'management–of–learning' bridge

Here the focus is very definitely on learning, and includes the explicit coaching of students to develop their own learning skills in the new learning environment. Children are acutely aware of the ways in which teaching changes as they move from one school to the next, as we shall see in a later chapter devoted entirely to the students' view of this experience in the middle years. What they are rarely offered is the chance to have these different expectations addressed head–on, with sufficient time devoted to helping them explore and come to terms with the implications of the different structures and methods of teaching they will now encounter.

Think back to the starting point of the Homerton College study, which I mentioned at the beginning of this chapter. The assumption was made that "we need young people who can sustain, through primary and secondary schooling:

- an enthusiasm for learning

- confidence in themselves as learners

- a sense of achievement and purpose."

Motivation, enthusiasm, confidence, feedback, goals, achievement—these are the heart of the matter if our students are to learn as effectively as possible. All that we do in our schools, and especially when the continuity of learning is threatened, should be based on these aspirations.

Just for a moment, think about the students you teach, and the school where you work. What do you actually do, explicitly and regularly, to provide these essentials for your children, and to sustain them as the children move on into a different learning environment or arrive with you from their previous school – or even from their previous classroom?

As we have seen, examples of school practice aimed at crossing the 'management–of–learning' bridge are hard to find. Some have arranged for teachers from neighbouring schools to learn together about new approaches to group work or student involvement in assessment, and then planned these approaches into teaching on either side of the 'divide'. Some secondary schools have devoted time in the first months of the students' first year to 'learning how to learn at secondary school', explicitly recognising and catering for the changes the students will face. In both these cases, teachers and schools have been prepared to invest time and energy in learning, rather than teaching, in the expectation that the investment will pay off for the students in terms of their confidence, motivation – all the things that help to improve results. These strategies are not an alternative to the pursuit of higher academic performance by the students, they are an effective means to this end – more effective than simply trying to teach more, faster, and assess for judgement rather than feedback.

I have devoted more space to the fourth and fifth of these five bridges because they are less familiar than the first three. Teaching methods and a focus on learning both penetrate deep into the practice and attitudes of teachers and students. They cannot be grafted onto existing practice and expected to work. They do not involve designing new forms, or going to meetings: they involve instead the hour–by–hour, day–by–day activities of teachers and students in the relative privacy of classrooms. They are hard to quantify, unglamorous, and don't provide photo opportunities. In the bustle of a market–driven society, they can be, and are, easily marginalised or ignored altogether.

Before moving on to consider the voices and views of students and teachers, one other area of contemporary educational research needs to mentioned here, although it does not specifically address issues of school transfer.

In 1988, Terry Crooks, a leading New Zealand educator, produced a review of the previous decade's research about the impact of assessment on classroom learning and students' academic performance. (The full research reference is given at the end of this book.) Terry's findings were clear and unequivocal: in order for assessment to actually improve learning, students need to be offered clear learning outcomes, specific constructive and regular feedback, a strong sense of involvement in the assessment process, and the opportunity to set and achieve specific learning goals. This kind of assessment is an essential part of learning, and has a major impact on the way teachers plan, manage the classroom, mark and grade work, and relate to their students. In this respect the assessment strategies described in Terry Crooks' 1988 review correlate closely with the teaching and learning implications in the Homerton College study of 1999.

As a testament to Terry Crooks' seminal work, ten years on in 1998, Paul Black and Dylan Wiliam from King's College London, reviewed all the research published since 1988 on the links between assessment and learning. In the intervening decade, assessment had remained a very hot issue, reflecting the prevailing global political interest in 'outputs' and 'value for money', especially in the public sector services. Drawing on hundreds of research studies published all around the world, the conclusions of Black and Wiliam were almost identical to Crooks' ten years earlier. They found little or no evidence that high–stake mass student testing, with all its implications for teaching and learning, did anything to raise the performance of students. It provided plenty of data about learning, or at least about the testable bits, but did not actually improve it. The assessment methods most likely to improve student performance were those which affected the motivation, confidence, feedback and goal–setting of the students. Sound familiar?

Black and Wiliam's findings do not underestimate the logistical and other difficulties teachers face in making some of these assessment methods work. Planning for learning has to replace planning for coverage; assessment for feedback has to replace assessment for reporting or ranking; students have to be given and to accept responsibility for their own learning, which many students find scary and difficult and will avoid if given the choice. In the middle of their study, the authors note, "Many researchers are puzzled by teachers' persistence in using assessment methods which do not appear to enhance learning." They may be puzzled, but many teachers won't be, because we have tried in our classrooms to use those methods of teaching and assessment which have been shown to have the most positive impact on learning, and we understand how really hard they are to manage, especially given the constraints of the systems and structures underpinning 'traditional' secondary schooling.

The combined effect of these three major research studies is overwhelming. Over twenty years, with evidence from different countries, different stages of education, different subjects, the messages are consistent. The only people who can improve learning are the learners, and the only people who can improve teaching are teachers. What matters is how these two groups of people work together, every day. Changes in administration, budgets, systems, and policy may have occupied an extraordinary amount of public funds and public attention, but they do not of themselves change the essentials of learning and teaching.

Much of what the researchers tell us is neither new nor surprising. It's main worth is to validate and underpin the best instincts of the finest teachers, to give them the confidence to persevere in the face of distractions and to share their strategies with their colleagues. School leaders too need such confidence, to give their teachers the encouragement they need to tackle difficult classroom issues, and to provide the climate of learning which teachers need just as much as students.

One big question

In what ways does the structure and timetable of the secondary school influence teaching?

Chapter Three:
The Students' Perspective and its Implications

For those who believe that educational research is a precise science, gathering the views of students has always presented problems. Questionnaires rely heavily on the attention the student is able to give to the questions, and their interest, capability and confidence in responding by ticking boxes or writing. Children weigh their words, both written and oral, less precisely than we might wish. Their responses in interviews may be affected by contextual factors such as the rapport with the interviewer, or the dynamics of the group, or the anxiety caused by being talked to in private. The choice of students to interview can radically affect the outcome, as it can with any form of sampling. Objectivity is even more of a problem when children are involved than it would be normally.

The views of the students simply cannot be ignored when we are considering learning and the impact of various events and circumstances upon it. Only learners can improve learning, and only learners can really tell us how it is for them. We cannot think for them or speak for them: the students must have their own voice.

The Homerton College study cited extensively in the previous Chapter drew on research revealing the student voice and perspective in the United Kingdom and in North America. To add a further dimension, this chapter will look in more detail at three southern hemisphere studies. One was published in 1997 by Denise Kirkpatrick from the University of Technology in Sydney, Australia. Students' views were also gathered in 1998 and 1999 from interviews with Year 8 and Year 9 students in eleven Greater Wellington schools, New Zealand. These interviews were conducted by Jenny Poskitt of Massey University, for the Assessment for Learning and Progression Project, which was funded by the New Zealand Ministry of Education and directed by myself. The third study also emanates from New Zealand, from a study of multi–cultural schools in the poorest areas of South Auckland, conducted by Jan Hill and Kay Hawk of Massey University, Albany Campus.

Denise Kirkpatrick's study combined questionnaires with follow–up interviews of a group of students during their last year of primary schooling (aged 12) and the first year of secondary. Drawing from previous studies (including many of those cited in Black and Wiliam, 1998) the interviews were designed to explore student perceptions of the reasons for academic success and failure, which in turn affect their self–efficacy – that is, their belief in their capability to improve. "Learners who attribute success to high effort and ability and failures to lack of effort generally perform better than students their successes to some external cause such as luck and their failures to low ability." The difference in these attributions is in the degree of control which can be exercised by the learner. If the 'locus of control' for their performance is completely beyond their reach, such as luck, or accidental differences between tasks, the student's intrinsic motivation declines: it will rise if the learner feels some control over the factors which affect their performance.

The most telling outcome of this study is the differences in attribution between primary and secondary students. Over half of the primary students attributed success to effort. This may reflect the culture of many primary classrooms, in Australia and elsewhere, in which 'trying hard' and 'having a go' are encouraged and rewarded. A smaller proportion attributed success to luck, or accidental circumstances of some kind.

When these same students were interviewed at secondary school, these proportions were reversed, giving the external causes of performance more emphasis than the internal. If students were successful, they explained this by saying that the task was easy. In some cases, they said, this was because they were just repeating things they'd learned before at primary school. If failure was the outcome, this was attributed to luck and other accidental factors. Occasionally, students claimed that getting the task in on time was more important than completing it properly.

All this is bad news for secondary educators. The students in Kirkpatrick's study commented frequently that they had done tasks before in their previous school, and that the work was too easy for them. Some students were annoyed about this, as it showed that their teachers had low expectations of their academic capability.

Another finding suggested that students attributed success and failure to chance because they really didn't understand the criteria used to judge their work. This might have been because criteria had been explained but had not sunk in, or because the criteria had not been shared by their teachers. "The students commented that at primary school they believed they had a clear sense of what was expected of them but this was not clear at high school."

Kirkpatrick concludes by suggesting some basic steps that could be taken to overcome the change in attribution which seems to coincide with the move from primary to secondary learning:

- secondary schools need to examine for themselves if there any features of the school which encourage students to deny responsibility for their own learning, and to see if these can be amended

- manageable strategies to this end would include making sure that students understand what criteria will be used when academic tasks are being judged, and that students also understand the instructions for successfully completing the task

- more time will be needed for learning and evaluating different approaches to new tasks and problems

- classroom environments should encourage students to see and share the work of others, and to to develop an understanding of expected standards.

Jan Hill and Kay Hawk's work in South Auckland schools added a further dimension, this time about primary teachers' practice in the months before transfer to secondary takes place. For some of these children, poverty, poor prior learning and a lack of academic success in the extended family have already loaded the odds against future academic success. Many of them already understood this, and their expectations for themselves were low. Their teachers want their students to be prepared for change in the new school. They tell them that the pace will speed up, the work will be harder, the teachers less forgiving, and public exams based largely on ranking face the students less than three years after transfer.

However well–meaning the purpose, and however accurate the picture of life in the secondary school, for some students these warnings merely confirmed their worst fears. Before ever encountering the new school, they expected to fail, and would perceive the first signs of difficulty as evidence of the beginning of the end. Almost all students encounter some learning hiccups in the first few weeks or months of the new environment: what matters is how they react to them. Confidence to seek help, and that it will come right in the end, provide the perseverance needed to get through the problem. If that confidence is already lacking and is now eroded even further, children give up quickly and then enter a downward spiral of difficulty, failure, inattention and possible disruption from which it is increasingly difficult to break free.

Neither of these studies mention another piece of 'confidence–busting' practice. It may be more apocryphal than real these days, but all of us have heard tales of the secondary teacher (or even the Headteacher) who informs the new students (and their parents) that all the children's previous learning counts for nothing and 'the real learning starts here'. For children who have faith in their abilities this announcement may be unnerving but represents a challenge they think they can rise to. For children whose 'self–efficacy' (ie belief in their ability to learn) is already shaky, this can set them even further back, facing a hill which looks just too steep to climb without the support of what they had learned before.

Do any of us say these kinds of things any more? If so, why on earth do we do it? Recognition of prior learning is one of the cornerstones of successful continuity. How can we justify not only a failure to recognise prior learning, but the inference that it was worthless?

The Assessment for Learning and Progression Project Interviews

This project involved eleven schools in all, including four secondary (Year 9 – 13, aged 13–18), six Intermediate (Years 7 and 8, aged 11–13) and one all through primary school (aged 5–13). Each school was asked to nominate a reasonably random sample of about twelve Year 8 or Year 9 students. These students were interviewed in small groups by a professional researcher who is particularly skilled and experienced in talking to children and young people. Just a few weeks before the end of the school year, Year 8 students were asked about what they were looking forward to in their new school, what they expected work to be like there, what they wanted their new teachers to know about them, how they wanted to be assessed, and if there was anything about moving to the new school which worried them.

Some clear trends emerged from the Year 8 responses. They were looking forward to the newness of it all, new friends, new uniform, new 'subjects' and choices. More than half of them said that they expected the work to be harder, with Maths and Science mentioned most frequently in this category. Physical Education was a major attraction for nearly half the students. A large majority wanted their new teachers to know about their learning strengths and needs and to act upon them. They wanted to be given work which was 'not too hard and not too easy'. This was the highest consistency of response of all the questions asked. On the assessment side, the Year 8 students wanted assessment to help them do better, and didn't like end of year exams. They were very clear that assessment should help students know how to improve their work and help teachers see how to teach them better. Only a few children said that the purpose of assessment

was just to provide information for the teachers, or to frighten students into working harder. Clear trends emerged about what worried the Year 8 students most. In descending order of importance, three key factors were getting lost, making friends and being bullied, and potential learning problems especially homework.

For the Year 9 students interviewed at the same time, towards the end of their first year at secondary school, the start of high school already seemed a long time ago. Getting lost and making friends, which had loomed so large a year before, now seemed easy in retrospect. But over half the students were very critical of the classroom experience, commenting on the strictness of the teachers, the amount of homework, too much teacher talk, too much writing, work that was too easy or too hard, adjusting to different teachers' expectations. The Year 9 students were as hostile to big end of year exams as their younger peers, but they seemed to have lost the plot about the purpose of assessment after a year at secondary school. Only five or six students now identified the purpose of assessment to provide feedback, and improve learning and teaching. For the rest, they either weren't sure what assessment was for, or assumed it was about making them work harder.

When they were asked what advice they would offer to incoming Year 9 students, the veteran Year 9s were full of homely wisdom. Keep on the right side of the teachers, listen to them carefully, work hard, don't wag lessons or fool around, wear your proper uniform or bring a note. They urged a positive and constructive approach to new subjects and experiences, keeping out of trouble, being yourself rather trying to follow older students, and trying your best. If teachers present such messages to students, the inevitable response would be, "Well, they would say that, wouldn't they." How much more powerful is the same message coming from the students themselves.

Implications

What are we to make of all this? What are the implications for teachers and schools of the perceptions offered by the students?

1. The students are most concerned, before transfer, about the social and environmental changes they face rather than those involving learning and teaching. 'Feelings are facts'. If those are the students' feelings, then we must deal with them seriously, or expect these issues to be unhelpfully distracting, particularly in the first few weeks or months in the new school. A student who feels very insecure and anxious is unlikely to learn well. All sorts of strategies are possible here, and schools are getting better and better at helping with these concerns. Heaps of suggestions and examples can be found in the final chapters of this book.

2. Most students are ready to see a variety of adults and encounter a greater variety of learning 'contexts' by the time they approach transfer to secondary school, but we should not expect them to cope with a huge change in teaching organisation and style all at once. It should be possible to plan the transition from primary to secondary organisation by stages. For a year or so, either before or after transfer, students might meet four or five teachers each week rather than ten. They might move around to specialist areas but still have a physical base they can call their own, and a safe place to keep their books and belongings instead of carrying everything around with them. They will enjoy the stimulus of a range of teachers but still be carefully monitored by one person who has oversight of their learning across the school, close contact with individual students and their parents/care-givers, and a clear role to act as the 'friend' of the student in dealings with other teachers. If these strategies are to work in a secondary school, they will cut across many long-standing attitudes, systems and structures. The barriers to change which these

51

represent should not be under–estimated, but neither should they prevent a more student–centred approach to the organisation of learning and teaching which students deserve as they make the transition from one stage of their education to the next.

3. Planning for teaching the incoming cohort of students in the secondary also needs review, if we are really listening to what our students are telling us. They want, expect and deserve tasks and standards from their new teachers which are 'not too easy and not too hard'. This sounds straight forward enough, but it is fraught with difficulties. Here are some of them:

    • The child's previous teacher is the best source of advice about the learning needs and potential of the child. The logistics of transfer, however, create difficulties when the new school receives students from a large number of schools and teachers, all of whom have idiosyncratic ways of expressing what they know about the child. In order for information to be guaranteed to be useful and used, providing and receiving teachers need to talk to each other in some depth to establish what the one is willing to write down and the other willing to read and act upon. These conversations are frequently frustrating because the two 'parties' are wary of each other, rarely understand each other very well, and are given precious little time to work things out between them.

    • Many primary teachers are convinced that their secondary colleagues will not read information about individual children's learning needs. They believe, at best, that the structures of secondary teaching do not allow individual needs to be catered for, even if they have been identified. At worst, primary teachers feel patronised or even ignored by secondary teachers, who – they feel – regard themselves as better educated (because they are 'subject specialists') and superior to teachers of younger children.   The resentment caused by this can undermine even the most professional approach to gathering and communicating information about their students' learning

- The academic snobbery which bedevils teachers' professional relationships has more anecdotes and stories surrounding it than we've all had hot dinners. For reasons we can only speculate about, there seems to be a view that our intelligence and professional capability is a function of the age of the students we teach. From this premise, educators in higher education, while highly competitive with each other, will unite in despising their peers in the high school. High school teachers in turn will look down on primary colleagues, and those who teach in the early years and in pre–school environments are patronised the worst of all.   This attitude is both absurd and deeply unhelpful to students making their way through their education. Like most attitudes, however, it is slow to change, and can be an insidious and troublesome barrier to the pursuit of a more sensible approach to primary–secondary transfer, and all other transfers, come to that.

- If information about learning is provided by the previous teacher, it will be several weeks out of date by the time it is read and acted upon in the early weeks of the next school year. It may well be necessary to spend a little while gradually recalling and reviewing learning which took place before the break. It certainly makes no sense to assume that if the children cannot instantly recall their prior learning, this proves that the prior learning has never actually happened and that the records are inaccurate.

- In the first few weeks of the new school some children are quite overwhelmed, by the size and complexity of the school, by making new friends, by the number of adults they have to deal with, by the travelling to and from school and coping with a host of other new routines. All this is on top of the annual re–adjustment to school after the long holiday. Some schools, however, insist that they will test the new students during the first few days to determine ability groupings for the remainder of the year. To some extent, this urge to 'get organised' is understandable, but the validity and reliability of 'first week testing' is highly questionable. Tests generate results, and these results can be used to 'place' students and plan for their learning, but if the results are themselves an inaccurate reflection of the capabilities and potential of at least some of the students, serious questions are raised about this practice. Surely, with all our professional experience and collective intelligence, we can do better than this.

Here's a horror story about first week testing. It happened thirty years ago, but the person who experienced it, now a secondary teacher with radical views about secondary practice, remembers every detail.

Ann attended a well–regarded girls' high school in a New Zealand city. She had come from a small rural primary school and was very impressed by the size and history of the school, and the beauty of its buildings and grounds. She was bright and excited about the new experience.

On the second day, all the new girls were summoned to the school hall. They were told not to talk as they entered the hall, where single desks and chairs were laid out in rows. Ann was overawed by the size of the hall, the biggest room she had ever seen, and by the huge honours boards hanging on the wall which named the Head Girls for the previous fifty years. She whispered to her friend and pointed out the things she had noticed.

Immediately, a teacher called her out of the line. As a punishment for talking Ann was told to take the test sitting alone on the stage, facing the other hundred or so girls in the hall. She was overwhelmed by embarrassment and managed hardly any of the test. On the basis of the test result she was placed in the lowest ability group, despite evidence from her previous school which would have contradicted such a placement. Ann was too embarrassed to tell her parents at the time, and is angry about it to this day.

Of course, that was a long time ago.

- By whatever means, teachers will discover enough about the starting points of the students to be able to plan appropriately for them. But what if the teaching plan for the first year is already fixed, based on certain assumptions and so rigidly tied to a time frame or to given resources that the teacher cannot amend it sufficiently to meet what she now knows to be the needs of her students? Or what if the teacher simply does not know how to adapt teaching activities to make them accessible to a wider range of learning skills and styles than she had originally planned for? What's the point of finding about prior learning if you cannot or do not act upon the information?

Recognition of prior learning is inextricably linked to differentiation, – the adaptation of teaching plans to meet the identified needs of individual students – which is a major challenge for the mainstream secondary teacher teaching around one hundred and fifty students every week.

4.   A further implication of the views expressed by the students concerns the ways they work with their new teachers. The students are used to working with one teacher for most of the time. They have grown used to the methods and routines of this teacher. Communication between teacher and students has become more efficient through long–standing familiarity. The students know each other well too, and know who to ask if they're not sure about something.

Now they are faced with several teachers each week, none of whom they know well or know them. The routines and ways of explaining things vary considerably from teacher to teacher. Students are keen to please and to do as they are asked, but sometimes they simply don't understand the teacher's instructions, and are unclear about her expectations, and the criteria by which the quality of their work will be judged. The students ask for the teachers to be more patient, to explain things more carefully, to make sure the students know and understand what's expected of them. This need will probably be temporary, while the students adjust. It may contradict the teachers' need to set strict parameters for clear classroom control and a 'tight start' to the year. 'Don't smile before Christmas' was the advice offered to me as a young teacher, although I could have fulfilled most of the students' desired teacher behaviours without smiling much. (In the southern hemisphere, where the school year coincides with the calendar year, the advice of course is 'Don't smile before Easter').

• Questioned about assessment methods, the students wanted assessment to give them specific information about what they were doing right and what they needed to improve on. This is the obvious concomitant of their desire to know the criteria, and the two fit naturally together.

- The students wanted some at least of their learning to be fun, and the teacher to be even-tempered and not moody or grumpy. They didn't want to be 'shown up' in class, when they're still not sure about their new classmates and often very self-conscious. Sarcasm from the teacher is the worst treatment because it is designed to humiliate.

5. Lastly, the concern about Homework. Many students in our sample were used to being set homework, but this was set by the one teacher they were familiar with. There was no chance of different homework expectations clashing with each other, because it all derived from the same person. Moreover, this person knew the child's capabilities and circumstances very well, having had sole charge of them for a year.

The children had all been warned by their teachers that secondary school expected homework to be set and completed every night. For some children, the whole issue is a nightmare. Their home circumstances simply do not lend themselves to quiet study at home. Home may overcrowded to the point where the child does not have a quiet place to work; family responsibilities for some children push homework to the edge of their concerns; some parents feel that school is for school work and home is for the family and the family's commitments, to the business, to older relatives or younger children, to church, or to the mosque.

Faced with these conflicting priorities the children are caught, and quickly learn to react to the strongest pressures upon them, whatever they may be and whatever the consequences of not fulfilling some of the school's requirements.

Life is made even more complicated for all children if they do not know in advance what homework will be expected by each teacher, and what the deadlines will be. Some schools will plan a homework timetable which dictates – or attempts to – which teachers and subjects will require homework on which night, to ensure that the workload is reasonably evenly spread. In other schools, the suggestion of a homework timetable is regarded by teachers as an unwarranted intrusion on their professional autonomy, whatever headaches it may cause the students.

The amount and nature of the homework also worried the students in the Wellington study. Many families will have experienced the problem of the homework task which turns out, perhaps through a misinterpretation by the student, to be a family problem lasting half the night. The homework task, the same set for all the students in a mixed–ability group, is simply too much for some of the students to tackle without help, and beyond the capability or experience of the adults at home who try to help if they can.

Sometimes the teacher uses homework as a means of finishing off tasks not completed in class, so that the class can move on together. But the student who didn't finish the task in class, and now has to do so at home may need the very help which is not available to him at home. Meanwhile the student who has sailed through the classroom task and clearly needs something more challenging is left with no homework at all.

It's always been a problem. Some parents demand homework and lots of it: for others it's a puzzle why school learning can't be completed at school. Setting homework appropriate to each child's needs is even more difficult than catering for these needs in class. Homework needs to be checked if students are to be motivated to complete it, which makes even more marking for a hard–pressed teacher. If the homework does not involve writing, then some parents and students think it's not 'real' work......and so it goes on.

Of course it is useful for students to learn and practice academic work outside the classroom, away from the immediate availability of help. But for students in the first few months of the new school environment it can drive a further distance between those who are coping and those who are not. Much of the difference derives from the difference in parental support for the child at home, which is already a major factor underpinning the success or otherwise of the child at school.

Could we find a better way through this minefield?

A year on: 'Give Up or Catch Up'

Looking a little further ahead, some months down the track in the new school, students speak of a choice which faces them as the serious business of exams confront them in their senior secondary years. By now they feel quite at home socially at school. Fears of getting lost have faded quickly, and instead of being overawed by the size of the place, and by size of the older students, they are now becoming those 'bigger kids' themselves.

Now for some of the students comes the growing realisation that they are falling further and further behind. For a while, early on in the new school, they were too distracted by the novelty of the big school to either know or care that this was happening. Their teachers may have taken weeks or even months to understand the right standard of expectation for each student. If the student was of a mind to do only what was required of them, and no more, their standards have slowly but surely been slipping away. Some primary teachers in our study certainly believed that some secondary teachers' expectations were too low perhaps because they confused writing skill with actual capability.

When the student begins to realise that he (and this most common with boys) has a problem, he also has to decide what to do about it. This is where the student's belief in himself becomes so crucial. If he believes that with help he will make progress, then he will probably find a way to get help. Often this will be from other students, but teachers should also look out for the signs that a student wants to 'catch up' and isn't sure how to do so. Adolescents sometimes have difficulty articulating what they want, and particularly so when they want help. Teachers who listen to and watch their students carefully will probably pick up with clues, and then find a private opportunity to check them out.

Other students facing the same realisation about falling behind will react differently. It's almost as if they expect to lose track of school learning, and have just been waiting for it to happen. Failure at school may be the repeating pattern in the family and regarded as something no one has any control over. "My Mum says she could never do Maths either, and not to worry about it". Parents sometimes collude with these low expectations from a desire to protect their children from the anxiety and frustration of raising their sights, because they suspect the effort will be fruitless, and they want the child to be happy. As parents, many of us have faced this dilemma, and have to struggle with it in our own way.

These may be the students who decide, unconsciously often, to 'give up rather than catch up'. They may continue to attend school, to see their friends and enjoy the activities, but they have actually given up. They are already 'truanting in their heads' although they are still in the building. Others again will give up more completely and sustain their self–respect by overt rejection of school and all it stands for. They pursue their satisfaction elsewhere, as far away as they can get. One or two teachers may even be relieved to see the back of them, and the increasing disruption they were causing.

'Catch up or give up'. That's the choice many students face, and the one we need to help with as carefully as we can.

A school anxious about its students' performance in public exams decided to take action. At the beginning of the exam year teachers were asked to identify those students they considered were achieving well below their potential. The school would then plan a campaign of serious intervention, involving the students themselves and their parents in direct regular contact with senior staff members.

One of the senior teachers involved reported what happened when the group of under–achieving students was brought together for the first time. Several of the students reacted in a way he described as "It's a fair cop, Gov'nor". They were not surprised to be there. For other students, this was a wake–up call they had not been expecting. These students, again mostly boys, had been 'cruising', giving just as much effort as was needed to 'get by' and nothing more. Our informant reported that these students were clearly shocked to be among the group. They looked around the room and saw who else was there. They looked at each other. They said nothing at the time, but each of them later sought out the teachers they expected to help them and asked, privately, for help. They wanted that privacy to be respected, because they feared that the decision to 'catch up' might damage their reputation for being 'cool' and their teachers wisely accepted the need to keep the new arrangement to themselves.

For some students, well into their adolescence, the social pressures they perceive – whether they are real or not – can make them behave in a way which they know is damaging to their own school achievement and future opportunities. It's a cycle they find it hard to break out of, and it starts as a reaction to moving to the new school. Puberty plays a role here of course, but the worst excesses of its impact on young people are relatively short–lived. If we can support them through it, and then pick them up again when it begins to wear off, the decision to catch up rather than give up may still be salvaged.

Checking your own students' views

The reactions of students in schools far away from yours, in different circumstances, may not provide you with evidence convincing enough upon in your own school. If you, like me, believe that the students' perceptions are a vital part of the picture, then you may want to check them out for yourself.

To do this well takes time. If it's not done well, it's not worth doing at all. You need to know a little about sampling: as a rough rule of thumb, less than thirty students might not give you the depth of information you need. You'd need to decide too whether to take a random sample – say one in five from the roll – or to focus attention on a more particular group, for whatever reason.

Having established the size and composition of the group of students you wish to question, you will then need to think about the method to use. Questionnaires are quick and therefore cheap, but it takes skill to design a good one, and to ensure that all the students fully understand the questions and are encouraged to provide the information you really want, to help you improve your practice.

Interviewing children about their views and suggestions will generate more useful detailed information, but here again you need to think carefully about the number and complexity of the questions, as these will largely determine the answers. It's worth considering also to whom the students' responses will be presented , and what they would be most interested in. The whole point of the exercise is to motivate the school to consider and act upon at least some of the views of their most important 'clients'. This may mean changing long–established practice, or challenging some assumptions among teachers, school managers, and even parents. Why not ask a group of these interested parties to help design the questions, or take a role in conducting the interviews? Alternatively, the interviewing could be done by a disinterested outsider, to improve its reliability, or by an influential and interested insider (perhaps a Governor with the time, interest and skills to help), to improve its impact.

A decision will be needed about interviewing students in groups or individually. For reasons of manageability you might prefer to use groups. It's also true that the conversation within the group can provide more information than might be provided by one child alone. To ensure that all the students are encouraged to contribute, you might want to limit the group size to three or four students, depending on their age and confidence. Will you want to tape the conversations? If so, who will get the unenviable job of listening to all the tapes, not necessarily to transcribe them word–for–word but to pick out the key points, the frequency of things being mentioned, differences of response relate to gender, or whatever the information is that you most want?

It's an 'action research' project, conducted by the school, in the school, to pursue issues and questions raised by the school, and with the responses used, along with other data, to inform changes in school policy, or simply to confirm the effectiveness of the existing practice. The Wellington experience reminded me of the power of the words and ideas of the students themselves in helping teachers to review and even to change what they do. It was a necessary reminder to all of us about the impact teachers have on their students, whether they aim to or not.

It is the teachers themselves – their aspirations, their activities, their frustrations – who are the focus of the next Chapter.

One big question

What do you think your students feel about moving on to a new classroom, or a new school?

Chapter Four:
The Teachers' Perspective and its Implications

For me, this chapter represents the heart of the issue. The attitudes, activities and goals of classroom teachers are the most central determinants of the experience of the students in those same classrooms. Policy makers, administrators, Principals, researchers can all express their views and exhort change, but if that call for change is not heard, accepted and acted upon by classroom teachers, nothing changes at all, not really. "You can make policy without teachers, but you can't make policy work without teachers ...." how many times have I been reminded of that wisdom since it was first expressed to me by a senior civil servant in New Zealand many years ago.

This passionate belief in the power of teachers to affect students' learning experiences may not be very proper for someone attempting a more objective research exercise. But it would be fruitless to pretend that I don't have such beliefs, or to let them prevent me from gathering useful information from teachers about the issue of primary–secondary transition.

In the final stages of the Assessment for Learning and Progression in New Zealand I decided to do just that – to interview a sample of teachers from the eleven schools I had been working with, individually and at length. I asked the same questions of all the teachers, and recorded them to leave me free during the interview to follow things up, to encourage further reflection and how the next steps they had suggested might be actually implemented. I regarded the exercise as an opportunity for professional development as well as fact–finding. The teachers willingly gave 40–60 minutes of their non–teaching time to me, at a busy time of the year. Some of them said they enjoyed the opportunity to think and talk about important professional matters, and to be listened to intently. Such opportunities were rare, they said, and much appreciated. Not for the first time I wondered why we do not pay more attention to the views, experience and professional intelligence of our classroom teachers, who are all highly educated and able people, and whose daily behaviours matter so much in our schools.

What the interviews could not show explicitly was whether and to what degree the teachers' attitudes and activities had changed as a result of my work with them. But that was not the first purpose of the interviews anyway, and involvement with the Assessment for Learning and Progression Project (ALP) was only one of several categories I drew upon to create my sample of teachers. I wanted to see a cross–section of teachers, and used the project schools because it was so much easier to deal with schools that knew and trusted me. Teaching experience within the sample ranged from five years to thirty. There were more women than men, especially in the pre–secondary group, but this reflects the gender balance within the schools as a whole. In the secondary schools, I tried to focus on the English, Maths and Science departments, and to include others who were suggested by their Principals as particularly thoughtful, or who had a special responsibility for transition in a pastoral capacity. Almost all the pre–secondary teachers in the sample were teachers in Intermediate schools. Some of these taught Year 8 classes, and some composite classes of both Year 7 and 8 students. Most of the intermediate teachers had taught younger children too at some stage in their careers.

Some explanation of Intermediate schools is necessary for non–Kiwi readers. Intermediates are two–year middle schools, catering for Years 7 and 8, which began in New Zealand in the 1930's and are now the norm in most conurbations, and less common in rural areas where children stay in the primary school until the end of Year 8, or right through to Year 13 in 'Area Schools' in the most isolated parts of the country. In both primary and intermediate schools the normal school structure is one teacher, one class,(with specialist technicraft teaching provided separately) and most intermediate teachers gained their pre–service training as primary teachers, rather than by the secondary route of specialist subject degree followed by one year's teacher training. There was only one 'full' (ie upto Year 8) primary school in the ALP project.

Another factor to consider is that until 1997, primary teachers were on a completely different collective contract than their secondary colleagues, paid at a lesser rate, ostensibly because they were not necessarily graduates. This clear contractual distinction had been a source of resentment and conflict between the two parts of the profession for many years, and it will take a while before the memories of inequality fade. One more special feature of the New Zealand context is the existence in this relatively small country of only one teacher union for 'post primary' teachers and a different union for primary and intermediate teachers. Probably because of the contractual differences, the relationship between the two unions has been strained at times, and few if any joint campaigns or activities have taken place. There is, as yet, no organisational common ground between pre–secondary and secondary teachers. The local subject associations which could bring teachers together are largely dominated by secondary teachers, or have faded away over the past few years because of the greater pressures on teachers' time and energy. This may be one more reason for the lack of communication between the two groups of teachers.

These factors are all pertinent to what follows, but the particularities of the New Zealand system do not – in my view at least – mean that these teachers' views and concerns are unique to New Zealand and have no relevance elsewhere. During the past decade I have been fortunate to work closely with teachers in various parts of the world. I taught in England for ten years in secondary classrooms myself, and for one year in an American high school (with 3,700 students!) and have enjoyed daily contact with schools and teachers from all phases and stages of the service since 1982. For me, these teachers' voices are trans– national. You the reader will need to decide for yourself whether they represent a reality you recognise.

Each of the teachers in my sample is a fine professional, committed to students and education each in their own ways, even if those ways are not identical. None of them occupies any moral high ground. They may be puzzled by each others' practice, and sometimes by their own, but there is no doubting their shared desire to do the best job they can for the students they teach.

For the purposes of this Chapter, I have divided the questions and the teachers' responses are divided into two main sections. First I asked about their perceptions of how teaching in the 'other' phase of education differs from what they themselves provide. I also asked where these perceptions originated – with interesting results. The second section deals with the teachers' thoughts about the barriers to learning at the time of transition from primary/intermediate to secondary school. In the final stage of the interviews I asked teachers for their views and suggestions about how these barriers might be reduced if not removed: these suggestions along with many others will be offered in the final chapters.

Secondary and pre–secondary teachers' perceptions of each others' teaching.

Here are some direct quotations from interviews with secondary teachers. You'll notice that the students are frequently referred to as 'kids', which I have left alone in the interests of authenticity, although I know some of you may not like its use.

- "Secondary and Intermediate schools are different branches of the same firm.... we need to get over the old jealousies and forge much closer links, and with the Primary schools too. It will mean establishing trust first, and then the mechanisms." (School Counsellor)

- "This is very prejudiced, I know, but I often feel that the 'eyes' of the curriculum are picked out at Intermediate school..... kids get the fun things but not the draggy old boring things that we have to do. Very few kids get a real grounding in Language." (Head of English)

- "Intermediates tend to do more 'touchy–feely' types of learning – group work, 'think,pair,share', artistic presentation, – secondaries just don't have time." (Head of Science)

- "I tried to use Cuisenaire rods with Year 9 students, and they said, 'We don't want these, this is baby stuff.' Playing is an important part of learning: concrete operational needs are not met in secondary schools." (Head of Maths)

- "Editing and proof–reading in pre–secondary seem to be about making the work neater rather than better." (Head of English)

- "Intermediate kids are busy, doing set work, but there's no encouragement to go outside the parameters of the teacher and the task.....that may be because of the insecurity of the teacher." (Head of Maths)

- "Because I have a certain ability in Maths I find it hard to imagine teachers who aren't confident with Maths." (Maths teacher)

- "Generally in Science, they've done all the cool stuff and neglected the theory." (Head of Science)

- "It looks like Primary teachers are keen on telling the kids what they can do and not honest enough about the weaknesses." (Head of Science)

- "It's much harder to establish classroom routines when the kids see five or six people in a single day." (Head of Science)

- "I do feel for the kids and what they face when they leave Intermediate, but we feel helpless in the face of all the things we're supposed to be doing and chasing the Holy Grail of School Certificate." (Head of English)

(N.B. There are plans to change the nature of School Certificate shortly, but it will remain as a high–stake event in Year 11 which will have a 'backwash' effect on the earlier years of the secondary school, as it does now.)

- "We pretend that we will instantly know these kids better than their previous teachers, which is rubbish." (Head of Maths)

The pre–secondary teachers had this to say – here again I am quoting directly from their interviews:

- "I have the impression that what primary teachers do and think is vastly different from what happens at secondary. Primary teachers try to **teach**, secondary just **present**." (Year 8 teacher in a full primary school)

- "Primary trained teachers just seem intuitively to know what to do with kids – how to talk to them, use groups, use a variety of resources and so on, – maybe because they've never had to teach to tests." (Deputy Principal, Intermediate school)

- "Secondary school teachers confuse poor literacy skills with poor capability. They underestimate the potential of the students." (Intermediate teacher, whose early career was in secondary schools)

- "It's not surprising secondary school is subject–oriented – the secondary teachers haven't had a chance to learn about how to be teachers...... it's ridiculous." (Intermediate teacher)

- "Maybe kids connect subject teaching with 'growing up'." (Intermediate teacher)

- "I would feel guilty saying to a kid who wasn't reading well, 'Don't worry, your teachers will always have something for you to do' – because I'm not sure that they will." (Language-coordinator, Intermediate school)

- "Secondary teachers deny responsibility for kids' learning beyond their own specialism – like when the kids can't read the stuff in Science, but they say that's the English department's responsibility…..it's ludicrous." (Intermediate teacher)

- "The kids have a certain identity here but over there it's just like cattle, constantly moving on." (Intermediate teacher)

- "Kids in Intermediate school have teachers who encourage and motivate them – all of a sudden that's gone." (Intermediate Science Co–ordinator, Science graduate, secondary trained)

- "It was mostly, 'Come in, sit down, here's some notes, practice a few questions, do some problems, here's the Homework,see you later'." (Year 8 teacher, commenting on his observations of Maths teaching in a local secondary school)

- "Why don't they let the kids make things in secondary school? Maybe they don't have the cardboard or something.... probably the 50 minute teaching spell makes a difference." (Same teacher)

- "I can't envisage secondary kids working in groups." (Intermediate teacher)

- "What does my impression of a secondary classroom look like? A couple of posters on the wall if you're lucky, and all the desks in rows." (Intermediate teacher, consistently critical of secondary teaching methods)

- "The secondary teachers say, 'It's different for you', but how different can it be?" (Intermediate teacher, after a visit from a secondary teacher to her classroom.)

- "If we had a more positive mind–set about kids going on to College [ie secondary school] we might do more to prepare them... it's hard because we don't know enough and we're a bit sceptical." (Intermediate Professional Development Co–ordinator)

If these comments leave you with an impression of a gulf in mutual understanding between secondary and pre–secondary teachers, often in schools just a few yards apart, you'd be right. For some years there have been virtually no direct dealings between them. The Assessment for Learning and Progression project had involved more encounters, and some shared activity, but still many of the teachers were unsure of what happened elsewhere and puzzled by what they were discovering. To fill out the picture in their minds, they drew from memories of their own school days, even twenty or thirty years before. Critical mutual stereotyping was the norm, good information was rare, and a non–judgemental acceptance of difference was even rarer. Blame was in the air, even while the need for closer liaison was being articulated.

As part of my analysis of the interviews I looked for the frequency with which certain responses to some of the questions were mentioned. On the question of the origins of teachers' perceptions about the 'other' phase, around 50% of the pre–secondary teachers mentioned that their perceptions came from their own experience at school, and acknowledged that they were therefore probably out–dated and coloured by some strong and often negative memories. For the secondary teachers, their perceptions came mainly from 'contact with pre–secondary teachers'(mentioned by 70% of the respondents) but not from seeing them teach. Only three of the sixteen secondary teachers interviewed had been in a working pre–secondary classroom in the previous year or two. For the pre–secondary teachers the number was one out of twenty one. For both groups, those who have children at school have been influenced, understandably, by the experiences of those children.

In one large secondary school, two key people – the Guidance team leader, responsible for liaison with neighbouring Intermediate schools, and the Head of the English department – had worked at the school for nearly fifty years between them, and neither of them could remember visiting a working Intermediate classroom within the past twenty years. One had been aiming to do so for six months since we first discussed it, but other more pressing issues (usually concerning continuing changes in the exam. system) had constantly taken priority.

The teachers' views about 'Barriers to Learning' at transition.

I needed first to establish whether the teachers believed that transition did create barriers to learning for a significant proportion of the students, not just the odd one or two. Out of the thirty seven teachers in total, only three felt that there wasn't really a problem, and all three came from the same pair of schools. The Secondary and Intermediate school in this case were only a few yards apart and the great majority of the Intermediate students went straight 'next door' to continue their education. The social disruption involved in these circumstances was considerably less than in other schools with more confused patterns of transition.

For the remaining thirty four teachers, transition from Year 8 at the end of intermediate or primary to Year 9 in the secondary school did present barriers to the children, although there was no clear unanimity about the nature of these barriers. 75% of the secondary teachers mentioned that the main problem is that the students are 'socially overwhelmed' in the new environment. This factor was mentioned by only 25% of the pre–secondary teachers, who more commonly ascribed the problem to secondary teaching methods, puberty, the 'loss of security', or peer pressure to be 'cool'. When asked about which children they would expect to thrive or to struggle in the new school, about half the pre–secondary teachers mentioned contact with home, or the decline in this contact, as a factor in successful transition, or not, compared with only three or four of the secondaries.

This data about the 'frequency of mention' came, it should be remembered, from entirely open–ended questions. Interviewees were not given a list to tick, or a series of yes/no responses. It made a nightmare of the analysis, but I'm still happier with the validity of the outcomes – fuzzy though they are – than I would have been with any other method of enquiry.

The range of factors mentioned by secondary teachers as potential barriers at transition was huge – thirty eight factors in all were mentioned at various times. Those that were mentioned more than five times included:

- the more rigid structures and formal climate of the secondary school (8)

- some new students being disruptive and demanding attention (5)

- puberty and being 'cool' with new peers, especially among boys (8)

- the overriding need to 'fit in' with peers (5)

- changes in teaching and learning strategies (8)

- learning not respected at home and parents 'give up' (6)

- secondary school teachers see too many students, and lose the personal contact the students have been used to (although this can return in the senior years) (6)

Some of the most telling and illuminating analysis of the difficulties faced by students and their teachers in the first year at secondary school came from the teachers themselves:

- "Somewhere in Year 9 you see the bright–eyed child transmogrify into the person who just looks at you and shrugs"

- "In some of our schools, 'It's cool to be a fool'. Some of our kids get rotten role models from the older students."

- "The student who asks a lot of questions is more likely to succeed, but the formality of the new school inhibits them."

- "For some kids, the change to secondary school is an organisational nightmare."

- "For some of our Samoan students, being part of the group is more important than individual achievement."

- "When they come and see round the school, we give them a 'magic show' in the Science labs, but that's not what real Science is about. We start them off with boiling water and more mundane stuff."

- "Some kids have multiple minor clashes with different teachers throughout the day, and these gradually turn into major trouble."

- "By the time we've got a good picture of the Year 9's as learners, the year is half way through."

- "The pace of change for senior secondary requirements is so fast that you end up 'punch–drunk', and this pushes the junior years lower down the list of priorities. If we could really focus on Years 9 and 10 it would make the later years much easier for us."

- "It doesn't sound good when you say it out loud, but maybe we know they'll be OK by the end of Year 9 because they spend most of the year repeating things they've done before."

The primary and intermediate teachers mentioned the following factors five times or more, out of a total of twenty seven factors mentioned:

- changing teaching strategies (7)

- declining rapport with teachers (6)

- puberty and the distraction from learning (8)

- fragmentation of teaching into subjects (5)

- the sheer size of the new school (5)

- loss of sense of security and being 'looked after' (5).

For this group, comments about difficulties in the first year of secondary school were more circumspect as they were further away from the actual experience. Some of their comments reflect their own management of students new to the Intermediate school, and how that must correspond to the secondary transition.

- "If you're given stuff to read every lesson which you just can't manage, your self–esteem just collapses"

- "One of my kids came back to see me after a week at the high school and said, 'I've had five detentions already because I keep asking what to do.' "

- "I teach the same kids every day, and even for me it can take most of the first term to re–establish a good learning environment to the point where you can really teach rather than just manage behaviour. When you only see the kids for a few periods a week that must take even longer."

- "Some kids still need 'morning talks', even just once a week, to let the social stuff out before you start working."

- "By this age, the kids are far more concerned about friends than about academic things. It's hard for them to break away from their friends if they need to."

- "If secondary teachers can't reach down to where the kids are at, the kids are failing before they start."

- "The social side of school can be a battering experience and self esteem is so important..."

Teachers' views about the information to be passed from pre–secondary to secondary teachers about the students.

Within the ALP project, we spent hours on this question, exploring the advantages and disadvantages of various strategies. Sometimes it felt as if the details could never be resolved until and unless the teachers understood and trusted each other more. Once such trust is established really difficult issues start to look so much easier.

Let's pick it apart into its respective bits, and identify the advantages and disadvantages of various strategies.

a)   What kind of information?

- about what the child has been taught

- about what the child has learned and can do

- about 'academic' skills, knowledge and understanding, usually identified within 'subjects' or 'areas of learning'

- about more generic learning skills and 'work habits'

- about personal and social characteristics

- about family background and circumstances

- about special learning needs

- about friendship groups, and which children needed to separated for their own good

- about health problems and needs

- about overall ability, relative to other students in the cohort

Some of these items are relatively non–contentious: everyone accepts that the next school needs to know a child's date of birth, address, health needs, where and how to contact the family in an emergency, previous school and so on. This is factual and essential to the school's duty of care. Beyond these essentials, the schools and teachers I have discussed these issues with over the years have a wide range of views which frequently contradict each other.

The New Zealand teachers in our project displayed a similar wide range of views. More pre–secondary than secondary teachers were interested in the individual children's strengths, talents and potential. Subject–related 'competence' information was wanted by 75% of the secondary teachers, whereas only 50% of pre–secondary had this as a priority. On the question of reading competence, 60% of the secondary teachers wanted it and only 30% of pre–secondary had it high on their list. Only 15% of secondary were interested in a statement about the child's personality, with a similar number feeling strongly that this would be too subjective and that the child should be allowed a 'fresh start' in the new environment.

Surrounding all these possibilities was a sense of frustration about the time it takes to write down all the information on each child, about the plethora of different demands made by different secondary schools, about the inconsistencies between different pre–secondary schools in completing the information. And at a deeper layer again was the pre–secondary suspicion that the next teacher was in fact unwilling to read what the previous teacher has said, and probably unable to use the information anyway because of the dominance of 'curriculum coverage' over 'real' teaching.

b)   How much information, and how arranged?

All the teachers agreed that information should be concise and manageable to both write and read, but when they began to talk in detail about what they wanted, keeping it concise became a problem. Making it look less by cramming everything onto a single sheet of paper was quickly dismissed as useless, as different pieces of information would be needed by different groups within the receiving school. Putting different things on different pieces of paper makes it seems like more, even if it's not.

Some Principals of schools and the people most interested in IT applications could see great potential in communicating between schools electronically. At first glance, the possibilities are attractive, but for a number of reasons I encouraged the schools to mark time for a while, to let the quality, validity and reliability of the information available catch up with the electronic potential.

Firstly, teachers would have to agree on the nature of the information to be gathered and communicated, taking account of manageability for both teams of teachers as well as doing justice to the students. Secondly, 'coded' judgements based on perceptions of achievement against certain criteria would have to be checked for consistency both within the schools using these codes and among them. Without such checks, the information might appear to be reliable, but in reality it was not. Thirdly, teachers would need access to the right hardware and software, or keying in the information might end up more time–consuming than writing it. Fourthly, we should never lose sight of the idiosyncracies and uniqueness of individual students by reducing them to data that suits the mechanisms of the software. Examples of a student's work, if needed, could be scanned into their individual file. The students themselves could create their own addition to the file in the form of a 'letter to the next school'. The more sophisticated school IT systems could handle all of this, but for those that cannot – at least not yet – the low tech. alternative of paper and pen has still lost neither its charm nor its effectiveness.

Why is information for progression always tricky?

No matter how sophisticated the technology available to us, the essentials are quite simple. Useful, agreed information about students needs to be identified, communicated and then used to assist their learning in the new environment. The potential barriers which could get in the way of this endeavour are the same now as they have always been, and will always be. Many years ago, when computerised records were merely a twinkle in someone's eye, this was my list of barriers: it's worth reviewing them every now and then.

- information about previous learning is not available, or not in time to be useful to the receivers

- information about previous learning is available, but does not include what the receivers really want to know

- information about previous learning is available, but is not considered to be 'trustworthy' by the receiving teachers

- school systems, the numbers of incoming students, and the number of providing schools all overwhelm the ability to see each incoming student as an individual with unique needs

- receiving teachers are either unwilling or unable to amend their teaching plans to take account of information about previous learning

- providing and receiving teachers don't understand enough about the next and the previous classroom or school to make sense of the information which passes between them

To some degree, these difficulties can plague us whenever students move from one teacher or school to the next: at the point of transfer from primary to secondary these problems are merely exacerbated by a number of other factors

c)   Student involvement in information transfer

The teachers were not asked directly about the possibilities of involving the students in 'presenting' themselves to their new school and new teachers. This issue has been dominated by administrative and bureaucratic considerations in the past, and therefore outside the realm of the students.

The suggestion that each student should be encouraged to 'write a letter' to their new teachers, as part of the information which accompanies them into the new school seemed at first to be an answer to a number of questions. It would illuminate the uniqueness of the individual student without asking teachers to write at length on behalf of the student. It would encourage students to think seriously about moving to the next school and the goals they wanted to pursue there. It would be a pleasing symbol of the centrality of the student, a refreshing alternative to the complexities of teacher judgements, form–filling and computerisation.

Beyond the initial idea, it was the detail – as ever – that made the teachers think more deeply about exactly what would happen, and what the implications might be. We had to start with clarity about the 'purpose and audience' of a student 'letter', just as we have to ask about purpose and audience every time a record or report is under review. In this case, we ran into a confusion straight away. Some secondary teachers were interested in seeing a sample of the student's unaided writing, from which to infer the student's writing capability which they believed to a major factor for success in many secondary classrooms. This could be a neat solution to two needs – learn something about the student as a person and have a preview of their writing at the same time.

We only had to look at this suggestion from the point of view of the student to see the flaw. If I was the student, I would want to present myself positively to my new school, in a way that made them see me as a real person, not just a 'writer', especially if I already knew that my writing could be criticised as untidy or inaccurate. The 'medium' of my writing would distract from the 'message' about me.

The two potential purposes of the student letter had to be dealt with separately. By all means, offer to the next school a sample of the student's unaided handwriting, as part of the picture of learning capability which the next teachers have to plan for. But let the student decide how they wanted to present themselves, so that the medium and the message could support rather than work against each other. The only restriction on the student might be a very practical one: their piece would be on one side of normal–sized paper, so that it could be copied for all their new teachers. If it was not easily copiable, the original would be in a file somewhere which teachers would have to go out of their way to find.

Alternatively, the student would keep the 'letter' and show it to their new teachers when they first encountered them. The student might prefer to communicate with the teacher privately rather than in public, especially a public of their peers whom they did not yet know and trust.

Of course, these ideas are not new for many schools. They follow logically from the idea of a 'Record or Portfolio of Achievement', containing items indicating the student's development, which have been selected and 'deselected' through a process of periodic review between the student and a personal tutor or mentor during their time at school. Such a process can – and does in some schools – start in the early years of schooling, and continue right through. When the process and the product are both working well, the Record of Achievement can be a central component of the information which accompanies the student from school to school.

On the question of involving the students, as with so many complex issues, there are no simple solutions which work well in the unique circumstances of every school. You can't just leapfrog into a new system without laying some foundations: in this case, the students would need to have some help and some practice in thinking about their learning and personal strengths, their needs and their goals before they would be confident to present themselves well. Parents too would need to be properly informed about what the school was proposing, and reassured about its purpose. And the teachers in the 'receiving' school would need to think about how they would handle the information offered by the students, constructively and with respect.

d) the timing of information transfer

The teachers could provide no absolute solutions to this problem either. They recognised that the long summer break from school has such an impact on some children's learning that good information gathered right at the last minute by the previous teacher might seem inaccurate for a while as the children adjust into school again at the start of the new year. Some period of adjustment and settling down would always be necessary, however well–informed the next teacher might be.

Those who arrange the groupings and schedules of the new cohort sometimes want information far too early. In some cases, six months or more might elapse between information being requested by the secondary school and the students actually starting work in the new school: in this case the bureaucratic needs of the 'system' are working directly against the validity of the information and its fairness to the students. The teachers in the 'providing' school can be left with the impression that the children are not expected to make real progress during their last six months, which is a veiled insult to them as well as to their students.

It looks inescapable, however strong the need for simplicity, that information will need to be gathered and used in two main stages, depending on the purpose of the information and the use to which it will be put. For administrative/ bureaucratic purposes some information will be needed in the last few weeks of the old year. Once the information is in school, access to it for classroom teachers may be delayed until the teachers are ready to look at it, which may be right at the end of the old year or in the few days of 'settling down' time which often precede the start of teaching in the new. Even if the new teacher is unable to absorb all the details of the learning capabilities of all her new students, she can clearly demonstrate to them an interest in what they have learned before, and use a more open–ended approach to tasks during the first few weeks to allow her to reach useful judgements of their needs based on some scrutiny of transfer records and careful attention to the students' approach to learning in the new classroom.

One Head of Maths talked in her interview about the timing of information for the department, and for herself as a class teacher. She would like access to some of the data about the incoming students' Maths 'levels' in the various 'strands' of Maths (eg. number, problem–solving, geometry) towards the end of the school year. This would give her and her colleagues the chance to look at the 'patterns and trends' for the incoming students, to review their resources and their appropriacy, to amend some of the time frames in the first few weeks of the programme, and to take note of particular students and their needs, at both ends of the capability spectrum. It would be part of the usual end–of–year review and goal–setting for the department.

For herself as the class teacher, the need and the timing were slightly different, she explained. She could look at individual children's records before she'd actually met the child, but the information didn't stick because it was 'decontextualised' and didn't relate to a 'real' person for her at that time. She preferred to scan the records for patterns and trends, and then see her classes for a few teaching periods, to get a feel for them as a group and as individuals, and to provide some fairly open–ended diagnostic activities to allow her to watch the students at work, to hear their 'talk about Maths' and to see what they could do, recognising the very different circumstances the students were dealing with. After a few weeks, she would go to the records from the previous teacher, identifying now with the name and face of each child. Now she could compare her early impressions with the information from a teacher who knew the child very well but hadn't seen them for about two months. She became aware too of children she had just not noticed yet, and made a note to herself to do so. All sorts of things struck her from the records which might not have done without some acquaintance with the children, however slight.

This was not 'fresh start' behaviour, rejecting the previous teacher's information as irrelevant or unhelpful. This was about helping her memory by providing some 'pegs of identity' on which to hang the information from her colleague in the previous school.

The nature of professional conversation: a cautionary tale

I saw recently another very interesting aspect of a secondary teacher's manner which affected some of her dealings with her pre–secondary colleagues, and I have noticed it among other secondary teachers too. Her manner and speech patterns were indicative of the rather worldly, sceptical and sometimes cynical climate of the large school in which she worked. Although the vast majority of the teachers were strongly committed to their students, it wasn't 'cool' to say so. Conversation sounded sometimes like a series of witty but fairly empty one–liners, designed to amuse or impress rather than to inform or explain.

Within the school, this way of dealing with people and issues wasn't necessarily a problem, except for visitors, or even new teachers before they understand how to glean real meaning from these abrupt exchanges. With other secondary colleagues, from schools with a similar climate, it was not a real problem either, except that now the derivation of real meaning was more difficult, and you had to try a little harder to understand fully what was meant rather than what was said.

In the pre–secondary school climate, this way of self–presentation did not go down well. Teachers' speech patterns in some of the primary schools were completely different, reflecting the different climate – or was it perhaps the other way round. Here, it was OK and expected to talk in detail about children and their learning. People were more explicit and careful with each other, less cryptic. Take this secondary teacher and place her in the primary school, or in a meeting with her primary colleagues. "Of course I don't look at the children's records," she said, without explaining fully the reasons why she would wait for a week or two, and the preliminary scan she and her colleagues had done earlier. She was a bright, sharp woman: no–one challenged her, and the explanation went untold. A series of unproductive exchanges took place in which she seemed – according to her listeners – to be bent on upsetting or shocking them. Again, nothing was said at the time, but the impression she left had obviously irritated the others, and confirmed their low expectations of the respect for their judgements in the secondary school.

I wasn't present at this encounter, but heard about it from both 'sides', and did what I could to patch things up. Ultimately, the liaison between schools cannot rely on the services of a 'broker' or mediator. Teachers and Principals themselves, as part of their professional responsibilities, need to develop the liaison with other schools necessary for trust, respect and good procedures to grow. The first lesson is about expressing yourself with care, listening hard to establish the way of thinking and the protocols of the school you are in and the teachers you are talking to. We have to start with positive assumptions about each other's motives and commitment to the shared task. With this starting assumption, when things which are done or said appear to be obstructive to the common goal, we ask for clarification. We might even need to explain that someone's way of dealing with us is causing confusion, and request that things are approached a little differently.

In a professional environment, our conversations with each other – especially in their early stages – must be guided by respect, high expectations, good listening and sensitivity. These are the foundations on which a real relationship can be built, with all its short–cuts and jokes and shared assumptions.

Prevailing Myths

Before we turn in the final chapters to the host of positive ways forward, let me take a moment to reflect on two of the myths most commonly encountered when the conversation turns to primary–secondary relationships. Both of these have affected our respect for each other for decades. They are out–dated, and need now to be recognised as unnecessary barriers to our mutual professional respect. We can do without them, and it's time we did.

Myth No. 1: "Primary teachers teach children – secondary teachers teach subjects."

The difference between primary and secondary approaches to teaching is often summarised as "primary teachers teach the child and secondary teach subjects". As a secondary teacher myself I was always unhappy with this as a generalisation. Earlier in this book I urged us to accept the complexity of the primary–secondary transition, and I think the time has come to get past this over–simplification. Yes, primary teachers are in continual contact with a group of children for a year or more and become acutely aware of the uniqueness of each child. Their role as the child's only or main teacher allows them to work through and beyond 'subject' divisions. They may well have been attracted into teaching in the first place by a passion for children rather than a passion for any one aspect of learning.

My own experience over the years has confirmed that many secondary teachers too are keenly interested in their students as young people, rather than mere recipients of the teacher's enthusiasm for a subject. They too may have wanted to teach for a host of reasons and the particular subject is for them the context for a wider interest in teaching. The continual stereotyping of secondary teachers as mere 'subject specialists', with all the negative connotations which attach to that, is unhelpful as well as being unfair to some. Similarly, the secondary stereotype of every primary teacher as a 'low–order generalist' with no interest in specialist subject matter, is inaccurate, unhelpful and unfair. It's all part of the blaming culture which we need to move beyond.

Myth No. 2: teachers in every new school want children to make a 'fresh start'

Logistical complexity bedevils the passing on of information about students to such a degree that sometimes the idea of 'fresh start' looks terribly tempting. Very occasionally, you come across teachers saying that 'fresh start' is the best positive choice for their students, but much more often teachers well understand that we need to distinguish between a fresh start in behaviour and relationships and a fresh start in learning. Even if the child has not encountered your subject before, no learner is ever a blank slate to be written on: the vast majority of the teachers I encounter are clearly aware of that, even if they find the implications outfacing.

The vast majority of school Principals and Head Teachers know this too. But in these competitive times, there are pressures to present your school as somehow completely different from what has happened before or elsewhere, and occasionally these pressures apparently override an educator's good sense. The research evidence about the need to sustain the confidence and self–efficacy of learners is now overwhelming: this surely cannot be served by publicly criticising or denying all previous learning. Parents as well as students need to feel confident that learning improvement is both possible and expected, without losing faith in what has gone before.

Is it just 'too hard'?

If the successful management of learning progression from primary to secondary was easy, we would have solved it by now. Getting it right with this issue is much more complicated than we may have wanted to recognise. It goes way beyond information gathering into some of the most fundamental and intractable questions which face us as a profession. Working in increasingly competitive environment, how do we foster a collaborative and positive climate among all the schools serving a community? How do we tackle the tension between the organisational needs of schools and the uniqueness of individual students? Why do we expect a mainstream secondary teacher to handle the individual learning needs of upwards of one hundred and fifty students every week? Why do we expect a pre–secondary teacher with thirty or more students in her class to be equally confident and skilled at teaching seven or eight specialist areas? How can we manage and monitor the learning of secondary students when the teachers who teach those same students never get the opportunity to talk to each other?

Of course it's not impossible, but it helps to be aware of the need to persevere, and to take a multi–dimensional look at the problem. To this end, in the final chapters of this book I return to the 'Five Bridges' identified by the Homerton College research team in their 1999 study. Taking these five categories of strategies, we will gather a wide range of experience and ideas. None of these can be seen in isolation. It's not a how–to checklist, more a way of stimulating the customised planning required in schools, both individually and as partners in a wider family of schools caring together for every community's children and young people.

One big question

In what ways, if at all, do you prepare your students for moving on to the next stage of their schooling, and/or induct them into it when they arrive?

Chapter Five:
Building the Bridges of Progression

As you will recall from Chapter Two, these five bridges each describe a category of strategies designed to enhance the learning progression of students from one school to the next. In this case we're looking particularly at the link between pre–secondary and secondary education.

The five bridges are:

1. The managerial/bureaucratic bridge

2. The social/personal bridge

3. The curriculum content bridge

4. The pedagogical bridge

5. The management–of–learning bridge

Of these, the researchers have already warned us, the first three present fewer difficulties than the last two, and the latter have the most positive influence on the quality of students' continued learning. Other research studies of the impact of assessment on learning have also alerted us to the powerful effects of assessment for feedback, involving the students as active partners in the review of their own learning and setting their own goals.

This Chapter is about suggesting ways forward rather than presenting the issue in all its daunting complexity. Before starting on the potential of even the first of these bridges, we need to state one basic premise. All these strategies need the foundation of a particular attitude of mind: all the parties involved must genuinely believe in the potential for learning and achievement of the students they share; they must accept shared responsibility, along with families and the students themselves, for developing this potential; they must avoid blame, and try to leave the baggage of the past behind. All this is harder than it sounds, as it may mean a change of attitude, which is more difficult than starting from scratch. Given these foundations, what does experience tell us about the first bridge?

The managerial/bureaucratic bridge

Meetings

Establish a pattern of regular but not too frequent meetings between the Principals/Headteachers of schools in your community. Where the community is hard to define, in densely populated urban areas perhaps where the patterns of parental choice have fragmented previous 'families' of schools, take a relaxed view of which schools might be involved in which grouping. Membership of a group does not imply that all your students will attend the secondary school in the same group. Indeed the purpose of the group may not be to manage all the individual students' progression from pre–secondary to secondary, but more broadly to keep all representatives of the various phases of a local service in touch with each other. They could do this by Email or by letter but a monthly or termly meeting is a good way to build trust and provide the clarity we need in the early stages of a good relationship. The details of the membership of such a group can be tricky at times, but don't let the details stand in the way of the idea.

Where the group meets seems to matter to people. So move the meeting from school to school, taking the opportunity to welcome guests to your school, to have a look round, talk to people, see children at work. If you feel the group needs leadership, and you don't have a 'neutral' person you can call on to help, move the chairing of the group around too, or agree that someone might have this role for a year at a time. Everyone there will have pressing demands on his or her time, so make sure you have prompt starting and finishing times, a clear focus of the meeting, and a brief written record of the outcomes.

It should be completely unnecessary to remind anyone about the protocols of an effective meeting, about listening, being respectful, keeping to agreed items under discussion. Here again, when we are involved with people we don't normally work with, like the teacher I described in the previous Chapter, we have to be especially careful about our assumptions. Different schools and teams have different ways of doing things: it may even be useful to clarify some basic ground-rules when you establish a new

group. You won't need them for long, but it gets you over the initial minor but frustrating hurdles.

When a group of fellow Principals gets together for the first time, they are understandably very aware of each other. The absurd hierarchies of education alluded to earlier can make us sensitive – maybe over–sensitive – to unintended slights. One of the unintended slights which can occur in a Principals' group is the decision by one of the members to send his or her deputy to every meeting, rather than attend in person. There may be good rational reasons for this: the Deputy has greater responsibility for transition; the Principal has 'more important' matters to attend to, or feels that s/he has been out of school too much lately. Deciding not to attend carries quite a message to the other group members, however, especially in the early stages of the group's development. The message may be interpreted as 'You feel you're more important than the rest of us,' or 'This issue is a marginal one for you'. If you commit to a group like this, as a way of building and developing important structures for your students, then commit to it properly, and re–arrange your priorities, until and unless the trust within the group is such that it can become a different kind of group, welcoming members not by status but by potential contribution.

In each of the schools represented in this group, the inference of the Principal's involvement is clearly seen by the rest of the staff. They will take their cue from what they perceive, and habit of constructive liaison with other schools can grow from there, encouraged with practical strategies as well as symbolic ones. Here are some suggestions.

- the administrative links between and among schools of different phases can oil the wheels of other strategies for putting teachers in touch with each other. Teachers visiting classrooms and teachers in a different school can be a formal part of a school's professional development or performance management system. It needs to be managed, rather than left entirely to chance and informal connections.

- the Professional Development Co-ordinators of a family of schools could spend some very useful time together, identifying the range of expertise which teachers in the family of schools can draw upon. Mentoring, 'critical friend' pairings of individuals or teams of teachers, a teachers' professional book group, shared action research – all of these need some administrative help to get them going and keep them going.

- once a reasonably trusting, no–blame climate is established, a group representing the schools might try to put together an agreed transition 'record' or 'portfolio', or improve on the systems already in place. This is harder than it sounds, juggling the various and sometimes conflicting needs of the various parties involved, but the discussion can help to build the empathy required for effective liaison, and the exercise is satisfyingly concrete for those who appreciate tangible outcomes.

- planning and managing a shared Professional Day across a family of schools serving different age ranges.

A shared Professional Day

Many education systems now specify a number of days each year which are to devoted to teachers' professional development. These days were not always greeted with acclamation by the teachers as they came out of what had been their holiday times, but once the dust of this change has settled, it can be seen what a great opportunity these days may provide for effective work.

Individual schools will naturally want to design their PD activities for themselves, but an occasional opportunity to work with teachers from other schools can be very valuable. I've had the chance to help with the planning and running of many days like this, where a family of schools agrees to work together, and what follows is a notional case–study of how such a day might work.

The Rutheby family of schools comprised the local comprehensive school, Rutheby High School, and five neighbouring primary schools, and a special school for children with emotional and behavioural difficulties. The Headteachers of these schools had been meeting at least once a term for the past year, and wanted to arrange a joint Professional Development Day, to focus on issues of both transfer from year to year, and transition from school to school. That was as far as they'd got, except to decide that the organisation might take quite a while to complete, so they had decided in their Autumn Term meeting in October to plan for the Friday before the Half Term break in October of the following year. That turned out to be a good decision.

Once the staff of all seven schools had agreed to the date, the next step was to establish a planning group to work out the purpose and structures of the day, possible invitations to outside contributors, and the main activities. Another early decision would need to be about the venue. Finding somewhere large enough for everyone but within the budget would not be easy.

Headteachers had already agreed that the planning group should not be run or led by them, although they would be kept in close touch. This was to be a day for the teachers, organised by them to meet their needs. Each school nominated a representative, and an alternate, to attend planning group meetings, which would be held at one of the schools where there was a good meeting room and enough car parking space for guests. At their first meeting they started with the first principles: what are the purposes of this day, what should be the expected outcomes and impact, and how can we arrange things so that these expectations are met, as far as possible? Then there would be some proper basis for the numerous decisions to follow. One or two of the seven representatives wanted to start with the venue and the lunch arrangements, but their enthusiasm for logistics was held in check for a while to ensure that the most important questions were tackled first.

The focus on transfer and transition was the first benchmark for their discussions. Only a small proportion of the teachers might be directly involved with the transition arrangements, after it was agreed that moving from one Key Stage to the next should be regarded as a transition, even if the children stayed in the same building. What about teachers who taught senior secondary option subjects and were not therefore so concerned with the junior secondary years? Could the same theme of continuity and progression be given a relevance for them through inviting guests from the local Further Education College, and an Admissions Tutor or two from the University? And at the other end of the age spectrum, it was suggested that representatives from the local nurseries and playgroups should be invited, to consider the importance of the transitions in children's early years, from home to playgroup or nursery and then on into full–time school.

Already the size of the group was growing, but if it made the day more potentially useful for every teacher, the small proportional increase in the total numbers would be worth it. So why not add a few more by inviting any of the seven schools' Governors who could find the time to attend? Agreed. Fortunately, the day was far enough away to give their guests plenty of notice, before their diaries got too crowded.

The temptation to have the whole group together for a major part of the day was resisted. It would make the organisation easier, but there was no chance that one shared experience could meet the range of disparate needs and interests in all the teachers. But there was a case for having one opportunity during the day for everyone to be together. Among the desired impacts of the day that the group agreed very early on was 'a shared positive experience, as a source of interest and conversation for everyone'. Clearly, there would need to be some opportunity for this shared experience other than just the lunch, however important that was deemed to be.It was felt that a short opening presentation might meet this need, but only if it was really good, and the presenter was well–briefed beforehand to make it as pertinent as possible. It should engage people, offer them some shared fundamental concerns and questions, encourage and motivate them and not last too long. The morning sessions are prime time in a PD day, and the group/workshop activities should not be delayed for too long. Above all, the presenter had to be skilled enough to be credible to an audience of two hundred professional communicators – the teachers themselves. If possible, all the guests would be encouraged to attend this first plenary session to give them a shared starting point with the people they would meet later. A short–list of possible presenters was drawn up, and two of the group took on the task of contacting them, in a descending order of preference. Once the presenter was identified, he or she would be asked to frame what they had to say round a number of key questions which would form the integrating theme for the day. One of these questions was, "What do we do to ensure that the needs of learners are identified, communicated and met as they move from one learning environment (classroom or school building) to the next?"

What do you think two or three other questions along these lines might be?

Now the day was beginning to take shape. An opening plenary, followed by the start of some practical focussed work together in small teacher groups, composed to reflect both a shared interest and a range of perspectives. The first workshop could start before the mid–morning break, for which drinks would be available at several points to save a lot of walking and queuing, and continue after it. Fewer longer blocks of activity were preferred to lots of shorter things, to give people a chance to get well into a task and to reduce the amount of movement around what would have to be a large venue to accommodate everyone.

At this point, well into the second meeting of the planning group just before Christmas, they felt they were ready to get into the logistical detail without losing sight of the professional purposes and activities. A suitable venue was found and booked, the likely costs began to emerge to be checked with the Principals' group, and the guests were identified, although not yet formally invited as the group was still not sure in every case what the guests would be asked to contribute.

At the third planning meeting, in early February, the organisation of the workshops was the main priority, and more people were invited to attend this meeting, to represent important phase groups who would be responsible for the organisation of these workshops. The early years people were quickly into their stride, working out the numbers of teachers and other colleagues who would be involved, how they use they had in both the morning workshop and another hour in the afternoon, before the final 'round–up' session, the details of which had yet to be agreed. The senior secondary group also started work, planning activities to interest and inform those who would be part of this group.

In the phases in between, two strands would run side by side, one looking at progression within the Key Stage, and another at progression from one Key Stage to the next. For the secondary people, the challenge was to examine students' learning 'horizontally' as well as vertically, with one group focussed on learning across Years 7 and 8 (the first two years of the high school) another focussing on Years 9 and 10, and yet another on the transition from Year 11 into the post–compulsory education and training experiences available to young people in the community. Subject departments at the high school had to decide who should represent them in each of these strands. For the small departments, this meant they would not be represented in some of the groupings, but that was the price to be paid for making choices, and the planning group were determined to provide a degree of choice, to share responsibility for the success of the group with the teachers rather than treat them like recalcitrant children. This proposed structure had to be checked with the Principals, and with the subject Co-ordinators and Heads of Departments, whose support was essential to making these workshops actually work.

The last decision made by the planning group was about how the day should end. It was agreed that some way of sharing key outcomes should be found before the details faded, although some more detailed write–up of the proceedings and the outcomes would be needed later. A final plenary just wouldn't work, they decided, but it might be good to bring everyone back together after the afternoon workshop for a break a drink, and to arrange the final activity of the afternoon.

It was eventually agreed that each workshop should prepare something visual to share one key idea or suggestion from their work together. These would be pinned on the walls of the plenary space, so that people could look at them while they had their mid–afternoon break. Finally, the teachers would meet for the final 40 minutes or so in their normal, comfortable groupings, to share what they had been doing and what they had learned and decided. So the primary and special school people would meet as a whole staff or in their Key Stage Teams, the secondary people in their departments or faculties. The senior school managers, who had been taking part in their chosen grouping during the day, would attach themselves to the most appropriate grouping for this session. They could lead the group themselves, or might have delegated it to someone well in advance so this person could work out a structure for the meeting. As an outcome of these final meetings, each grouping would agree and write down three action points, with as much detail as possible, to be shared first with the rest of their own school and ultimately be included in the write–up of the whole day, which would be the final task of the planning group.

End–of–day evaluations were widely regarded as a chore and not conducive to good reflection, so an evaluation format was worked out to be completed in each school within a week of the event. The action points agreed by each group would be kept and sent back to the group early in the Spring Term to remind them all what they agreed to do, and to monitor what they had actually managed to achieve. These findings would then be returned to the Headteachers' group for their consideration, and possible further action.

Most of it worked well, but there were a few glitches on the day. There needed to be one person from the planning group liaising closely with staff at the venue, not two or three people who kept bumping into each other. One of the Admissions Tutors was late, but fortunately the other was fine with support from a young teacher who demonstrated previously unknown skills of group leadership. They should have organised a creche in advance for those people from the playgroup who wanted to bring their children with them. The display of key ideas didn't work well because it wasn't close enough to where drinks were being served. The morning speaker went ten minutes over time, but they just delayed the morning break by ten minutes and that was fine.

Days like this don't just work by accident. The evaluations were almost all favourable because teachers felt that their needs had been met individually as well as collectively. The main complaints were about the vegetarian option at lunch, not enough air in the main plenary room, and one of the groups getting distracted from its task by an argument about something that happened three years previously.

Above all, and the hardest to quantify, the shared day recognised that the teachers in this family of schools were jointly responsible for the continuing learning and development of all its young people. They achieved a better understanding of each other by planning together, working together and eating together. In the future they might put a face to the name mentioned by a student or a parent. They might know who to contact with a question or a concern. They might trust the professionalism of the person from they were inheriting a child or receiving some information. We don't all have to like each other, but we need to recognise our common professional concerns, and respect each others' commitment and capability.

Shared Professional Development days, organised with the care that this one was, can take us a step nearer to that goal. They can also, incidentally, be a disaster. Can you spot some of the stages at which things could have gone badly wrong, if different decisions had been made?

The social/personal bridge

According to the Homerton College study, schools in the UK at least have improved their strategies for building this bridge in the last few years. A cynic might claim that this is all part of more careful marketing by secondary schools, anxious to 'sell' themselves to prospective students and their parents before the choice of secondary school is made. On the other hand, if this anxiety to attract students makes the school more approachable, provides more and better information about the school and its expectations, and makes the student more comfortable when they finally arrive there, what's the problem?

Problems really arise when schools put too much energy into marketing. Firstly, the marketing game can start too early, potentially distracting both students and teachers from the real business of the last year of primary school which is learning, not reading brochures and attending open evenings. For the schools trying to 'sell' themselves, over–zealous marketing distracts key staff from their core purpose too. Secondly, the game can get nasty and even damaging professionally, if schools try to gain an advantage over other schools – their 'competitors' – by making them sound inferior, and thereby damaging the confidence of those children who will attend them.

From whatever motives, we are improving our efforts to ease the child socially into the new environment, and every little helps when the children themselves tell us their fears of getting lost, of being bullied, and being overwhelmed by the anti–learning culture which many young people impute to their older peers, assisted no doubt by television and the all–pervasive 'culture of cool'.

Many opportunities for social bridges to be built occur before the child transfers into the 'big school', at whatever age.

Before transfer

1. Senior primary children, in the year or two before they transfer, can visit the local secondary school for some specialist teaching, or to use specialist resources which they would not

have access to otherwise. These visits allow them to see the school at work, to begin to find their way around, to check out the toilets, see some familiar faces among students who left primary the year before, and encounter some of the teaching and support staff. Even more impressive, to establish some positive role models in the minds of the younger students, is to encourage senior students to work alongside the younger ones, coaching them how to use specialist equipment for example, or explaining a skill area they may not have encountered before. These senior students may have been to the same primary school, or catch the same bus, or live in the same street. They have been an object of fear or mystery for the younger students, and now here they are demonstrating some of the joys the secondary school has to offer.

This need not be a whole–year commitment to have the impact of reducing the students' anxieties about working in a new environment. Most students adapt quickly once they can see how the new environment works: it's the not knowing that worries them most.

2. There are many other opportunities for visiting the secondary school, beyond the rather dry 'walk–about' which almost all schools organise for incoming students. If the schools are close enough together, after–school extra–curricular activities could be opened up to prospective students as well as existing ones. This could be a privilege for primary school students in their last year, in recognition of the important step they are about to take. Membership of a school band, or drama group, or Chess club, any of these will reveal the niche that an incoming student may need, especially those who may be less skilled socially. Some students revel in the larger social group which secondary school presents to them: for others it's a nightmare until they find some like–minded peers.

3. So far the strategies for building the social/personal bridge have involved the younger students visiting the secondary environment on a number of occasions and for a variety of purposes during their last year or two at primary school. Visits the other way can also be part of the plan, and have a variety of positive spin–offs for the staff as well as the students.

One of these is to enable secondary staff, if they wish, to spend a small proportion of their time in the pre–secondary environment, providing a specialist input which is not available there. Learning a second language is the most common focus of such a strategy. The secondary school is deliberately investing some of its resources – perhaps two teacher hours per week for each school involved, plus travel time – in the long–term 'engagement' of its prospective students. There will be children receiving this programme who choose in the end to go to other schools, and that's OK. All the children, at this burgeoning stage in their learning lives and before the major social upheaval happens, can benefit from a widening of their horizons, both personally and culturally.

Of course, the development of such a scheme must have the positive approval of the primary schools involved. They must regard the move not as 'doing a favour' for a neighbouring school, but as a definite enhancement of their students' experience. If the arrangement can be made to work for the benefit of both schools, the benefits to the students are easy to envisage and hard to quantify. They will know one more face when they get into the new environment. There will be one more person who knows them as learners and has seen them *in situ* in the previous environment. They have been expertly introduced to an area of study which in its early stages requires a positive attitude from learners, and an interest in other people, other countries, other ways of communicating.

The secondary school, too, benefits from a better understanding of its new students. The teachers have not only visited the 'partner' schools but worked there, picked up the talk in the staff room, offered information to teachers whose view of the secondary school may need refreshment. In this sense, the student–centred social/personal purpose of this strategy quickly merges into other very valuable links, for the teachers as well as the students.

4. So far we've looked at secondary visiting the pre–secondary environment to work with children, and get to know the teachers and the environment in which they work. A further purpose for a pre–transfer visit is to talk to parents.

I'm sure things have changed in the past several years in the way secondary schools approach their first contact with the parents of the incoming children. Traditionally, these took place on secondary 'turf', and included an address by the Headteacher, extolling the virtues of the school, stressing the need for hard work at school and at home, and – with equal emphasis – the need for the correct clothing to be worn at all times. Not so many years ago, I witnessed the Head of a boys' comprehensive spend several minutes explaining why boxer shorts were not allowed for boys in his school. The parents listened, eyes wide with wonder at his choice of subject from the stage on their first meeting.

It doesn't have to be this way, unless that's what we want of course. The pre–secondary school, in my experience at least, would be happy to invite the parents of its older students, and the students themselves, to come to school to meet the Head and other key people from the local secondary school, or schools. The surroundings are familiar and less daunting for some parents than the secondary school hall. They can see the respect and professional contact between those who currently manage their children's learning and those who are about to inherit them. The 'known' can mediate the introduction to the 'unknown'. Sometimes older students come too, to talk from their perspective about the opportunities they have experienced: not hype, just information, for both parents and the children who are with them.

5. Another primary school of my acquaintance took the unusual step (at least in the local context) of inviting representatives of the local secondary schools to come and meet parents before the families made their choice of secondary school, to explain how their schools managed the successful 'induction' of incoming students. Some of the schools mistook the purpose of the meeting, and began the usual preamble about the virtues of the school, the rugby, team, the uniform, and so on. "No," said the parents patiently, (this was a very affluent community) "we want to know how you are going to make our children feel at home in your school and ensure that their learning progresses smoothly." The schools had no choice but to respond, and very illuminating it was too, to hear the assumptions that were made about incoming students' needs. The most 'prestigious' school in the room implied that attending the school was a privilege for which both parents and children should be grateful, and that was that.

6   Another form of 'visiting' from secondary to pre–secondary can be through the students. Some social education programmes in the pre–secondary school may already have built–in suggestions: senior students are invited to talk to their younger peers about 'Saying No to drugs and alcohol', and resisting the negative peer pressures which the children themselves worry about. Students on work experience are often welcomed at the primary school.

7. In a previous Chapter about the students' perspective on transition to secondary, we heard the good sense and insight of the Year 9's message to the Year 8s about how to thrive in the first year at high school. "Keep on the right side of the teachers, don't let little problems get out of hand, do your homework, stay in school, take advantage of all the things the school has to offer." Enough to bring tears to your eyes! What a waste to have these pearls offered to the interviewer when they could have been offered directly from student to student.

Of course, there is always the anxiety that the pursuit of 'cool' and a degree of bravado might alter this message somewhat. Pre–secondary schools who have invited secondary students to talk to their leavers about what lies ahead will want a positive as well as authentic message to be offered, and will rely on the secondary school to select for this purpose students who will do a good job, without being dishonest. We know from our talks with the Year 8 students that they greatly value the chance to talk about 'what it's really like': however much they trust teachers, or any adults come to that, there is always the feeling, 'Well, they would say that wouldn't they.' Pre–secondary teachers who have invited in students, often past students of the school, sometimes find a reason to 'pop into the stock room' for a few minutes, to increase the feeling of a more private conversation among the children, trusting that the older students will be both honest and reassuring.

After transfer

1. After the students arrive in the high school, a variety of useful strategies are used to settle them in. Older students can be trained as 'mentors' and attached to form groups, individually or in pairs, to show them round the school, help with administrative details, answer questions, support and

encourage in any way they can. Some schools maintain this attachment for several weeks, or even the whole first year, although by the end of the first term many of the students don't feel the need for such help any more. What they may need by then is the chance to catch up on teaching which just slid past them unnoticed in the first few weeks, while they were distracted by other things.

2   Some secondary schools provide a special induction programme for the new students during their first few days. Together the students work through their 'Welcome to your new school' booklet, which explains all the day-to-day things they need to know about how the school works, who's who and what's where. Occasionally, the induction programme may address directly the differences in teaching and learning which await them, but more often than not these are explained by each new teacher, with no necessary coordination between them.

3. Very occasionally, the secondary school will take the opportunity to focus on identifying students' learning styles, asking about their prior learning, and looking at their Records of Achievement. Some students can find this a little unnerving in the company of others they don't know well. They worry about being exposed or laughed at, and may not be as forthcoming as their teachers might wish. If the students are relatively relaxed, and a good group climate has been created though the skills of their tutor, this early focus on learning can provide a necessary reminder that school is about working as well as meeting new people. We need to be honest with our students about what they will find hard as well as the 'cool' bits of their new environment. Above all they need evidence of high expectations, and encouragement that they can do it.

The Curriculum Content Bridge

National and provincial curriculums have been devised in many education systems over the past ten years or so, and continuity of content was one of the purposes they were designed to fulfil. Logically, it makes sense for all the children passing through an education service provided by the state to be taught certain things in common, which are arranged so that the content flows smoothly from one stage of education to the next. Unfortunately, however, in almost every case, the new curriculums were over-stuffed, so loaded with detail and threats about 'non-compliance' that schools were completely distracted for a while from the essentials of good learning. One impact of this rapid change in teaching requirements was to make teachers focus single-mindedly on their own slice of the curriculum in isolation from the others. They lost the energy it takes to look beyond their own patch, to what the children are learning before they arrived, or after they move on. In the secondary school, the priority for each department was to manage its own stuff: managing the overlap between subjects and departments was not a priority, to the long-term detriment of teachers' workload and students' learning. Liaison between schools actually declined in many cases, until the schools got their confidence back and began to rebuild their relationships, although by now these had often been contaminated by the perceived need for 'marketing'.

The dust cloud stirred up by the introduction of new required curriculums seems to last about five years, or less if the Principal/Head teacher is really clear and confident about how to manage the change process. When the dust clears a little, we can see more clearly beyond the confines of our own schools, and the possible advantages of finding out what's going on around us. In the secondary school, departments find ways of sharing their plans and expectations for cohorts of students, to ensure that connections are made if they would be useful and the students can make sense of what they're doing across the school as a whole. This is about building curriculum content bridges across different parts of the same school, and not before time.

There are a number of possibilities for sharing curriculum content between schools, to ensure smoother continuity of learning between them.

- The most simple strategy is to offer to the next or the previous school copies of the scheme of work or teaching plans which you have already drawn up for the students on either side of the 'divide' between the two schools. No extra work is involved: these plans already exist. For the primary school, this would mean sending a copy of the relevant parts of the Key Stage Two Maths scheme to the Maths departments in the secondary schools which most of your children move on to. In return, the primary Maths Coordinator asks for a copy of the Maths programme followed by children in their first year at secondary school.

If there is a degree of trust between the schools, and if the key people have actually met each other, these plans will be looked at with interest in the 'other' school. Questions will arise quite quickly: you may find unplanned repetition of key activities, and need to talk about how this could be turned into planned consolidation. If the plans include examples of tests or other assessment strategies, it would be useful to compare teachers' expectations. Exemplars of expected standards are also very useful for spotting where the discontinuities might creep in.

Once the plans on paper have been looked at and the questions identified, then it may be time for the Maths coordinators from two or three schools to get together with the secondary Maths department and talk some more. At the end of this chapter, I suggest an activity for such a meeting which focuses on the practicalities of task design, managing learning, making sound judgements, developing next steps, and so on.

- It may be possible for groups of interested teachers from the different schools to plan a shared task together, to be given to all the students they teach within a given week, and then to talk about how the students fared. Here again, the climate among the teachers will have to allow for this to happen without defensiveness and blame. It will reveal differences of perception and interpretation, but that's to be expected and is the necessary first step towards improving things. If the time frames for change are reasonable, and the workload implications tackled in relatively easy stages, then we feel we have enough control of it to sustain our motivation, assuming that the job is worth doing.

- Much has been written over the years about 'bridging units', topics or projects which are started in one school and continued in the next. The idea is attractive in some respects: for a start, it requires teachers from different schools to work together, pooling ideas, experience and resources. This may actually be the most professionally productive part of the exercise, a case where process is more useful than product. For the students, the message of continuity is a very powerful one, especially if the teachers can cross over during the course of the unit, with some secondary teachers contributing in the primary school and vice–versa.

The logistics of bridging units can cause problems when the secondary school draws from schools where the students have not been involved in the pre-transfer parts of the unit. In urban areas, where students by-pass the local school to attend one on the other side of town, or where a single-sex school draws from all over the place, there are few clear patterns of movement from primary to secondary school. In the first year secondary school there would then be some children who had started the bridging unit and others who had never heard of it: quite a challenge for the new teacher. The students who had not been at schools involved in the bridging unit could feel quite excluded from it, through no fault of their own. "It's not fair," would be heard almost immediately unless the teacher managed to handle the distinctions among the students very positively. To overcome these problems, each 'half' of the unit could be designed to 'stand alone'.

One final thought about bridging units, from the students' perspective. The students in the New Zealand research study said almost unanimously that they wanted their next teachers to know about and build on their previous learning. But they didn't necessarily want to 'cover' the same things. They were excited by the move into secondary school because it was different, although the massive differences they currently experience were just too much for some of them. Would they all welcome carrying on with a topic they had started in the previous school, even though it was only a few weeks before? Entry into secondary is perceived by many children as a 'rite of passage' after which they expect to be treated slightly differently because they are more 'grown up'. For some at least, the very continuity which the bridging unit is designed to provide could be a source of irritation. The purpose of a bridging unit is to motivate and engage the students: if it fails to do so because of their reaction to it, we might be better advised to focus on the continuity of teaching methods, not curriculum content.

Sharing standards, to achieve a greater understanding of the shared curriculum

In my work with teachers in various countries over the past few years I've been struggling constantly to improve teachers' understanding of each other across the structures of schooling which threaten to divide them. The introduction of new curriculums has provided an opportunity to focus on the outcomes of our teaching, which in turn has led us back to examine the necessary 'inputs' – our teaching.

In the United Kingdom and New Zealand, these expected outcomes have been described in terms of 'levels', and eight or nine levels are used for the full spectrum of learning from age five to around 16. In Canada, 'levels' have been defined within a year/grade rather across a band of years. There are advantages and disadvantages for those approaches. One advantage of the UK/ New Zealand approach is that it encourages teachers from different year levels to talk to each other about what they think these 'levels' actually mean, and what they look like in samples of students' work. This is necessary to improve the 'reliability' (consistency and fairness) of the judgements made by teachers

and reported to parents and to the next teacher. The Canadian approach to levels does not necessarily require teachers to share standards in the same way, because the 'standards' described relate solely to the curriculum described for that grade level, and no other. Progression can be measured within a year, but it's much more difficult to identify an increase in learning over a number of years.

So what? What's all this got to do with a better understanding between the teachers of different age groups? I want to explain an activity for teachers which I - and many others - began using several years ago in the UK as a means of 'standardising' (i.e. making more reliable) teachers' judgements of their students' 'level' of attainment within the framework of the National Curriculum.

At first we focussed on sharing standards among teachers of the same year group, or the chronological bands of years we know as 'Key Stages'. Realising what a useful professional development exercise this is, I started to use it with teachers from different Key Stages, and in particular those on either side of the transition between primary and secondary school. The rationale behind this was two - fold: firstly it improves the common understanding and use of 'level' as a short - hand way of describing a student's achievement; but secondly, and more importantly, it provides a structure for more fundamental conversation about the tasks we set students, how we support their learning, how we analyse and derive meaning from what they do, and how we use this to establish worthwhile next steps for them.

Some brief attempts to use this same approach in Manitoba have made me feel it's useful there too, even though the structure of levels is quite different. The first element of the rationale may not be so important, but the second still is. This is how it works.

1. Bring together a group of teachers from two or three different grade levels, and preferably from the years either side of the primary to secondary transition. You will need to agree to meet four or five times, for about one hour on each occasion if you are meeting after school. A much better option if the opportunity can be found is to meet twice, for two or three hours each time, at the beginning of the day rather than the end. These meetings can be quite demanding and work much better when people aren't tired after a full day's teaching.

2. The group may need some 'neutral facilitation' from someone who understands what they are trying to achieve, and can concentrate all their attention on guiding the group through its discussions.

3. Choose an 'element' of the curriculum which you want to focus on. Most people start with some form of writing, which is easier than starting with something less tangible and familiar. Then design a task which you will use to judge the students' 'standard' or 'level' of achievement, using the criteria described in the curriculum. You will need to decide whether the assessment task can be used as a free-standing piece, or be part of a teaching module. The task will have to be open-ended enough to be tackled with some success by all your students. Alternatively, only one age level of students will attempt the task, and teachers at the other age levels will help to judge the outcomes, even though though their own students have not been directly involved. There are advantages and disadvantages of both ways of doing this: you choose.

4. This shared task makes the discussion later about what the students have done easier, because everyone understands what the task is about. If you wish, you could side-step designing a task and ask instead for everyone in the group to bring in some samples of writing done by students in the normal course of their class work. If you do that be prepared for some potentially tedious explanations of different tasks before you can get to discussions about the outcomes.

5. Having done the shared task, or just with samples of writing drawn from the classroom, each teacher whose students are involved picks out one or two examples of what they think achievement looks like at the top of the range, at the bottom and in the middle. In the UK this would mean, for students in Years 6 and 7, picking samples to represent your view of levels 3, 4 and 5. In Ontario, you might be looking for samples of Levels 1–4 in Grades 6 and 7.

6. To make the group's discussion of these samples more manageable, let someone do some preliminary selection of the samples which will spark good conversation, and which will be easier to reproduce. It's a good idea to pick some items in which the child's handwriting and presentation belie the actual quality of the writing: a good piece of writing, but poor handwriting, and vice versa. This will generate the need for teachers to get past some of the cosmetics of children's writing which can be such a distraction. I'm not saying for a moment that the cosmetics of writing don't matter, but sometimes the criteria for judging writing are concerned with other things - the structure of the writing, its 'voice' for its intended audience, its impact on the reader, and so on.

7. The group has by now met once to decide on the task, the students have produced some writing, the samples for the group to look at have been chosen, and sufficient copies of these samples are made so that each person in the group can clearly see and and read them. You could put them onto overhead transparencies for everyone to see, but I find it's actually easier for teachers to have a sample in their hands, to make notes on if they wish.

8. Before you start looking at the samples, go back to the criteria for the 'levels' you are looking for and review what you think these criteria actually mean. What are the 'key words' in the level criteria, and how do these levels differ from each other, even by just a word or two? Don't get too bogged down in this exercise. The shared meaning will probably only emerge as you look together at what the criteria look like, not from the 'decontextualised' words themselves. Some of us have a tendency to get very picky about the meanings of words, which can drive other people crazy, especially at the end of the day. Your chairperson or facilitator will have to spot when it's time to stop looking at words and start looking at the work itself. You could go straight to the samples of course, but I've found it helps to clarify a few key words first, to avoid having to stop and start all the time.

9. When you start to look at the chosen samples, be prepared to slow down and look at each one really carefully. To add structure to your discussion, use the 'annotation form' on the next page, and complete the various questions as you go along.

These are the kinds of things that will crop up as you do so.

Identifying the student

- You'll notice that the name of the student is not called for, and the age and grade level can be omitted if you wish. This is quite deliberate for two reasons. Firstly, we are not talking about the student but about their work, and it's very tempting to start explaining the work in terms of the student's history, family, social behaviour, which can distract us from the focus on what the student has actually done. Secondly, we may want to use this sample to illuminate the nature of the required level or standard

Annotation sheet for a sample of student work

Age of student in years and months (if known) ▢▢

Grade/Year ▢

Context/Task
What was the student asked to do?

How much support was provided if any?

Which are the main learning outcomes involved in this task?

Analysis
Which characteristics of this work relate to which levels of the outcomes?

What else does this piece show?

Next Steps
On the basis of what you see here, what would be your next specific teaching step for this student?

to someone else - another teacher, or parents or other student and the identity of the author of the sample must be protected.

Even if we don't know the child , we can be distracted by the clues provided by the name about gender, family, ethnic or even socioeconomic background. In the UK, certain first names are commonly associated with particular socioeconomic groups - a curious remnant of the old class system. Just this first name can trigger expectations among teachers, and these may get in the way of an objective analysis of the work and what it indicates about the child's capability. I've seen it happen. Have you?

Context

- If you have used an agreed task, the first question, 'What was the student asked to do?' will be easy. If not, the teacher whose student's work is being looked at will explain the task the student was doing which generated this outcome. It's very hard to understand the work and its qualities without knowing what the student was trying to do.

How much support was provided, if any?

- Unless the task was done under very strict test conditions, with no intervention at all by the class teacher or anyone else, we need to know whether the child was given any help. Such help should not be regarded as cheating: it was provided to enable the child to show us what they can do. There's absolutely no point - for the child, the teacher or this exercise - in giving a child something they can't even get started with, and just watching them achieve nothing.

What are the main learning outcomes involved in this task?

- Here again, if the task has been designed to provide evidence of certain outcomes and standards, this question is easy. If an individual teacher designed the task, it helps us to know what we are particularly looking for. Our scrutiny needs a focus.

Analysis

Which characteristics of this work relate to which levels of the outcomes?

You'll notice here that I'm not asking which level this single sample of work represents. It's not useful or valid, I believe, to derive the level of a student's work from one sample alone. You have to look at the work over a number of occasions to make a valid judgement, not just one. The purpose of this question, about the characteristics of the work compared to the criteria, is to make us look more closely and carefully at the detail of what the child has done. It may be that some aspects of the work are at one level and some at another. That's OK, as the overall judgement we make will accommodate these variations and fluctuations from one piece of work to the next. For now, it doesn't matter: we just look for, talk about and record the characteristics we have noticed concerning criteria we are looking for. Less experienced teachers sometimes take longer with this than more experienced ones. Give people a few minutes to look at the work on their own or in a pair before you launch into whole group discussion, to make sure that everyone is able to take part.

What else does this piece show?

We can never pretend that everything important in a child's work is contained in the criteria laid down in a prescribed curriculum. Each child is unique, and we need to be constantly on the look out for the cues and clues about how an individual child's mind is working. So having looked for the things on our list of criteria, we now look for anything else that strikes us. Is there anything interesting here, in the content, the expression, the presentation, the spelling, the interpretation of the task, that we might need to check further or follow up with the child himself?

The child's teacher may be able to help us here, or we may notice things which the teacher has just got used to and doesn't notice so clearly.

Next Step

On the basis of what you see here, what would be your next specific teaching step for this student?

This question lies at the heart of teaching. If we want to move this child's learning forward, what are the one or two next things we would need to to do? These next steps are very specific and functional. They're not of 'Tell the child to try harder' variety. The useful next step will be more like, 'Go through with the child, and the others who need more help with paragraphing, how we decide when to start a new paragraph, and give some practice within the next few days.' Or, 'Check whether the child understands when to use a capital letter, or has just forgotten how to form upper and lower case letters differently.'

It's a bit daunting to have other teachers discussing your students and their work and what you might do next, but I've witnessed some very helpful and constructive conversations around this point, as more experienced teachers share the strategies they've developed over the years and the less experienced teachers just soak it up. Here are real teachers talking about practical ways of improving the learning of real children: these are the things which teachers need and want to talk about, and with the right structure and opportunity they get right into it.

If you only get to look at two or three samples of work in the course of a meeting lasting an hour or so, that's fine because the conversation has been about learning and teaching. When you do complete the annotation form for a work sample, pin the two together and keep them. They form the basis of a 'standards portfolio' which can be of great benefit to teachers, Head teachers/Principals responsible for the quality of teachers' judgements, the students themselves and their parents. Don't forget all the items in this portfolio will be anonymous.

How does this help students' transition from year to year and phase to phase within and between schools?

The 'traditional' groupings for teacher conversation about learning and teaching in primary schools have been related to the age of the students: early years teachers talk to other early years teachers, Year/Grade 5 to others from Year/Grade 5, and so on. The common ground for the conversations is provided by the age and stage of the students. In secondary schools, the common ground for teacher talk about learning and teaching is provided by the subject: teachers talk in departmental teams, about subject-related things. It's often difficult for both sets of teachers to feel comfortable talking beyond these self-created boundaries, especially when there's a whiff of blame and defensiveness in the air.

Conversations based around analysis of student work involving both primary and secondary teachers bring special tensions of their own. To be successful, the conversation needs both a structure and some guidance, at least in its early stages. It also needs a rationale when teachers' time is short and other priorities are pressing. Sometimes the rationale has to be extrinsic just to get things moving. It is necessary and expected in the UK and in New Zealand, that teachers using the 'codes' of 'level' in their calibration of students' progress from year to year and school to school will take steps to ensure that their interpretations of these 'levels' are consistent.

In Canada and other systems where levels are particular to each grade level, the first essential is that teachers within a grade level reach fair and consistent decisions about their students' learning to report to parents and the school as a whole. To encourage teachers to see this standardising as a 'vertical' (across grade levels) as well as a 'horizontal' (within a grade level) process may necessitate a wider view of the student's progress from year to year. Teachers need first to regard themselves as members of a team who each contribute to the learning and development of each student. From this starting point their interest and curiosity about what happens on either side of their particular grade level may increase, and needs to be encouraged.

Some will no doubt argue that teachers working in 'vertical' teams in the primary school should, and do, start with planning. You start at the beginning and only later look at the outcomes of what the children have done. It sounds logical to do that, and quite illogical to work the other way round. My own experience of working with teachers tells me that starting at the end, with the students' work, and moving backwards into planning from there really helps to sharpen the mind, and to reduce the gap between the planning process and the actuality of the classroom practice - between the rhetoric and the reality. Nothing is more engaging and stimulating for many teachers than what the students actually do.

Good guidance of the teachers' conversations, especially for a 'random' thinker like me, means that it's OK to jump back and forth between work analysis and planning as we begin to understand the connection between the two. Here's an example of how I've seen that happen.

> *A group of senior primary teachers, covering Grades 5 and 6, had been looking at some examples of students' written work. They had started by reviewing the expectations of*

high quality work as described in the Provincial curriculum. Looking at the work itself, one or two of the teachers seemed disappointed that some of their students did not appear to have reached this highest standard. Their own experience of the students told them that they should have done so.

"Hang on a minute" said one of the teachers. "Let's go back to the task we actually set the kids to do. Did it really encourage them to show all they know and can do, or did the task itself put a limit on what they could show us?" Sure enough, the wording of the task and the way it had been presented to them did not enable all the students to show all of what they could do. The link between task design and performance was becoming clearer. Then the teachers looked at the other end of the ability spectrum, and realised that the task did not enable children of more limited ability to show what they knew about writing in this mode either. If children with particular learning profiles had been restricted in this way by the task itself, could it be that the task was not enabling many children to do themselves justice? The teachers went 'back to the drawing board' on task design and task presentation, and they learned heaps.

When the discussion group includes teachers from different phases and schools, progress has to be a little slower because you keep bumping into things that some people take for granted and others don't. I remember primary teachers with a special interest in language meeting with English teachers from the high school. The conversation had started as we looked at some children's writing about the books they had been reading, and moved on from there. It became clear that the practice in the secondary school was for all the children to read the same book with their teacher, in the class, on which written work would then be based. The primary teachers looked at each other. "You mean you read the same text with all the kids?" said one. "Yes of course, what do you do?" "We let the kids choose, and then set written tasks based on each book," came the reply. There was silence for a minute while we all thought about this. No wonder the kids are sometimes puzzled by what happens when they move school: we are puzzled ourselves. Things are not better, or worse, they are just more different than sometimes we realise.

It's hard to anticipate all the issues which will arise when mixed groups of teachers look together at student work and analyse what it tells them about learning so far and next steps to come. Suffice to say that this focus has generated some of the most rich and interesting conversations between primary and secondary teachers that I have witnessed. Don't expect that they will produce instant enlightenment and the answer to all the challenges of 'Trust, Communication and Differentiation', but with perseverance, all these will definitely improve.

One big question

In your local 'family' of schools, which of your current strategies for improving progression is working most effectively, and why?

Chapter Six:
Two more Bridges – the Harder Ones to Build

Chapter Five looked at three of the five bridges for building progression, the ones to do with

- managerial/ bureaucratic bridges

- social/personal bridges

- curriculum content bridges.

The foundation of all of these is a degree of trust and cooperation between teachers and schools, but these three do not require a major change in the ways in which teachers teach and schools are structured. The fourth and fifth of the bridges identified by the researchers have more challenging implications, and deserve a chapter of their own. Some of the issues here were alluded to in Chapter Two, where I tried to take an overview of the structural issues, and of the most recent research into transitions, showing how formative approaches to assessment can influence both learning and teaching. The fourth and fifth bridges are:

- the pedagogy bridge

- the management–of learning bridge.

The Pedagogy bridge

The differences between primary and secondary approaches to teaching have been a continuing theme so far, expressed quite forcefully by the teachers themselves. Before we can look at how bridges might be built to span the divide, and smooth out the big steps which face students passing from one to the next, we need to explore a little further where these differences may come from. A number of factors may be at work here.

1. People aspiring to be teachers may find themselves attracted to one or other of the sectors because of their prevailing interests and attitudes, which may in turn have been formed by their own schooling, upbringing, and even their genes. One of the teachers spoke about primary teachers having an 'intuition' about what to do to help younger learners. If intuition is part of what makes a good teacher, this may propel the teacher towards one type of school or another.

2. The different ways we select and train our prospective teachers may also make a difference to the way they work. Until very recently, secondary teachers were nearly always specialist graduates who then decided to teach and received quite limited pedagogical training. Primary teacher training places simultaneous emphasis upon content – in a wider range of subjects – and on pedagogy. This simultaneity seems to lock the two together in the teacher's mind in a way which is quite different to their relative separation in the secondary teacher's mind.

3. In secondary education, especially in systems with high–stake content–based exams, the need to 'cover' the prescribed content to prepare students for these exams dominates the senior years of the school, and can also have a 'backwash' effect into the junior years. Planning tends to be for coverage rather than learning. Furthermore, assessment throughout the secondary

school tends to mirror the assessment approach used in these high stake exams. If these exams grade students comparatively, by ranking their performance against those of their peers, this determines the culture of assessment throughout the school. If judgement is based on comparing the students' performance against pre–set specific expectations, this approach will be dominant elsewhere. The primary assessment culture, traditionally, has assessed for progress, and to look for positive individual performance, although this is currently being affected by standards–based approaches built into the new curriculums. All these factors can influence the decisions teachers make about planning, classroom activities, assessment, marking, grading and reporting.

4. Finally, and the most visible difference between primary and secondary schooling, is the structure and organisation of teaching and learning in the respective schools. One teacher, one class is the norm in the first, with specialist teaching and students having several teachers is the norm in the second. Secondary schools tend to be larger and more socially diverse, although that is not always the case.

The interesting question is which of these factors has most influence on the differences we find in practice: interesting, not in the academic sense but because the answer should affect what if anything we choose to do about it?

As no definitive answer to the question will probably be forthcoming, let's look at each of these factors which underpin or reinforce pedagogical differences between primary and secondary in terms of practical strategies to bring the two a little closer together, at least where the two currently meet each other, in the middle years.

Strategies for closing the gap

We need to address the things that create different 'teaching cultures' in primary and secondary schools.

- By every means possible, raise the professional kudos of teaching younger children, to counteract once and for all the absurdity of basing one's professional standing on the age of the students you teach. Such an ingrained attitude will be hard to shift, but we have to start somewhere.

- Let's try and moderate our traditional deference to specialist subject qualifications. These alone do not, and never did, mean that someone can teach others effectively. Sometimes the best teacher is the person who has himself had to struggle with what he is now teaching. This may mean trying to persuade members of some appointing panels, and the communities they represent, that the possession of a PhD doesn't necessarily mean a good teacher. Of course we want well-qualified people to inspire our children, but it depends what they're qualified in. I happen to have a Masters Degree: I received it for producing a thesis on the relationship between the Czechoslovak Communist Party and the Czechoslovak trade union movement, 1945 – 1968. Pretty obscure stuff, and totally irrelevant to my ability to teach History to secondary school students, which was my first teaching job.

- Encourage and enable teachers to become better informed about current teaching and learning practice in schools and stages other than their own. Some of the myths about primary and secondary practice can only be changed through direct experience of each others' work, rather than relying on our own experiences as students. Minds need opening a little too, to stop us seeing only what we want to see.

- It should go without saying that beginning teachers need to paid sufficient to give them self–respect as well as a living. And while we're at the policy maker level, let's confirm that undermining the public's faith in teachers has a marked impact on the career choices of the brightest and best of our young people. Who would want to join a profession which has been systematically vilified? And nothing is more demoralising to a young teacher than a demoralised staff room.

2. The second potential source of pedagogical difference is the way we train our teachers.

   - Redouble the effort in current pre–service teacher training to balance the emphasis between pedagogy and content. Three years's content followed by one year learning how to teach is not the balance which will help any teacher, primary or secondary, do a great job with students.

   - Try to resist the inexorable current pressure to reduce the length of pre–service teacher training to make it cheaper and therefore possibly more attractive to students who now need to fund their own training. Learning how to teach is hard enough without expecting to cram it into a 35 week space.

   - As teaching becomes an all–graduate profession, we must keep struggling to ensure that the teaching qualification rests on the most relevant and authentic criteria we can find, however hard they are to assess.

   - Assuming that the pressures of market forces and other constraints will continue to affect the quality of those who are attracted into and qualified to teach, we must continue to regard this qualification as just the first step towards a longer apprenticeship. To complete this apprenticeship will require more training, mentoring and some degree of 'supervision' such as is required of colleagues in some other professions. Evidence abounds about the impact of teachers on their students, good and bad. Definitions of competence are now being reviewed to raise our expectations of ourselves and each other, which must be in the interests of all teachers collectively as well our students. These expectations now include regular opportunities for continued professional development, and the chance to tackle the issue of pedagogy for those already teaching as well as those entering the profession.

- We could make a list of all the desirable teaching methods we expect to see in every effective classroom, primary and secondary. We could put everyone through a rigorous and well–scripted in–service programme. We could exhort, threaten, and check. But teaching is mostly a private activity, conducted behind closed doors in the traditional egg–box design of many schools, at least many secondary schools. The only effective approach to changing the way teachers work will be one which takes full account of their intelligence, their instincts, their experience and their anxieties. Learning for teachers, as for any other learners, will need to take account of existing learning styles, prior experience and the learner's own perception of their needs. Expert mentoring will be part of this process, as well as culture of learning in the school for the adults as well as the children. 'The Learning School' will be part of the solution in improving teachers' pedagogy.

3. Changing the exam system in order to change pedagogy.

One of the most intractable barriers to change, or even the contemplation of change, for many secondary teachers is the dominant influence of senior secondary exams whose ostensible purpose is to select those young people who will most benefit from higher education, in all its various forms. "We have to focus on content, memorisation, formal writing and doing everything under time pressures," runs the argument, "because that's what the universities want, and they call the shots. If they don't change, neither can we without risking the future opportunities of our students. It's high stake stuff, so reliability matters more than validity."

I have to admit that at this point my patience begins to wear a little thin, although I'm not sure whom I should be getting impatient with. I cannot for the life of me see what writing four essays in three hours has to do with life in the twentieth century, never mind the twenty–first. Maybe I was away the day that truth was explained. Wherever the problem lies, and however hard it may prove to fix, fix it we must. It could be that the secondary sector manages through collective persuasion to convince their higher education partners to broaden the skills which give access to the most sought–after programmes. Or perhaps those sought–after programmes will themselves bite the bullet and realise that their selection criteria may be denying access to those who would benefit most and best fulfil the key outcomes of the programme.

Some years ago, I was invited to talk to the managers of a highly prestigious medical school about their dilemma over both the selection and training of would–be doctors. "We've come to the conclusion" they told me, "that by using senior school exam grades as the main selection criteria we are choosing people who will make good scientists but not necessarily good doctors. Then we train them to memorise huge amounts of detail which may be obsolete by the time they qualify and unnecessary and impossible to hold in the mind. Those who cannot or will not manage this memorisation are eventually required to leave. The ones who remain face their first clinical encounters handicapped by a big gap where their communication skills ought to be.

Many of them can't handle these new skills, for which they have been neither selected nor trained, but it's too late for them to leave now so they stay where they are to become doctors who are neither very good nor very happy." The shape of medical training has changed radically in the past few years, for reasons of cost–effectiveness rather than educational philosophy. Secondary school exam results overall continue to be a relatively poor predictor of future academic performance.

The nature and organisation of senior secondary examinations is changing slowly but visibly in the UK and in New Zealand. The implications of the changes do involve a wider range of assessment techniques and evidence of achievement, and greater involvement of both students and teachers. The backwash effect from the 'new' exams could be as positive for secondary pedagogy as the old backwash was not. With this leavening effect unfolding at the senior end of the secondary school, there are opportunities too for some greater flexibility at the junior end. The structures and pedagogy of teaching are unquestionably linked, and need to be perceived and tackled as parts of the same problem.

Changing the structures of secondary schooling, to enable pedagogy to develop

Knowing what we know about learning, it really makes no sense to fragment it into five or six separate bits every day, and thirty odd bits every week. Nor does it make any sense to continue to use comparative assessment methods which have been repeatedly shown to hinder the learning of all but a few students – those few who have confidence in their capability to be 'top'. To start both of these strategies, simultaneously, at precisely the same time as we face the students with major social change and the turbulence of adolescence....no wonder some of our students find it hard to adjust. It is a testament to the resilience of both themselves and their families that so many of them survive the change relatively unscathed. Two out of five students fail to make expected progress in the first year after the transition into secondary school, according to the researchers. That's just too many.

What is to be done?

- The changes in teaching and school structure may well need to change as the students move through the education system, but gradually rather than suddenly as at present. The number of teachers students encounter should gradually increase year by year, during the middle years. This process would begin in the senior primary years, or or in the year immediately prior to transfer. In larger schools, some small degree of specialisation or cross–grouping would enable students to encounter teachers they do not know so well, and to experience the learning strategies they need to manage this. In smaller schools the constraints of staffing make major change more difficult, but it is still possible to achieve some greater spread of teacher–student contact by periodically swapping classes, or putting two groups together with two teachers working with students they don't normally see.

- In the secondary school there would need to be a determined effort to change some of the traditional teaching structures. Encouraging and rewarding teachers to specialise in the junior secondary years, and to teach beyond their own main specialist area in order to reduce the number of students they encounter every week, would certainly be two steps in the right direction, once teachers' anxieties about career paths were allayed. Those appointing teachers to senior posts in schools would need to recognise the positive skills and experience involved in such teaching, and their relevance to successful school management.

- Having teachers teach two subjects to the same students begins to blur some of the boundaries between those subjects, and raise the interest of both students and teachers in learning rather than teaching. More emphasis may be given to 'learning how to learn', and to a wider range of teaching and learning styles which need more flexible approaches to time and tasks. By offering the option of more time on some tasks, and more flexibility in deciding when to move on, teachers can plan more varied activities without the intrusion of a bell and necessary movement every fifty minutes or so.

- Establish the junior secondary years as a rich and fertile area for teachers to develop their pedagogical skills and focus on learning rather than instruction. At this level, the connections between subjects can identified and managed, by both teachers and their students. Students' skills in time management, collaborative group work, self and peer assessment, review and goal–setting which have already been well–developed in the primary years can now be built on energetically, and the students convinced that these are the skills of the adult world, not just 'baby stuff' they need to leave behind.

- The connecting threads of essential skills, some blurring of subject boundaries and a reduction in the number of teachers encountered by the junior secondary students should all facilitate further structural development. Junior secondary teachers involved with a particular group of students should be recognised and treated as a team, encouraged to meet as part of the meetings schedule of the school, and to share their experience and ideas for effective teaching of their students. Leadership and career development opportunities can be built into the management of such teams.

- It should be possible to enhance the junior secondary concept even further by providing a physical base for the first year students at least, where they can safely leave their belongings, and where much of their teaching could take place. These teaching spaces might be more flexible than some others around the school, to allow a wider range of teaching styles to develop from the training which some secondary teachers benefit from. If useful training is offered to teachers but the physical and time constraints on them remain, there is less chance that the desired developments will take place.

- Provision of a space to call their own could be accompanied by the continuance of the responsibilities which many senior primary students enjoy and handle very successfully, and which stop abruptly when they become the youngest members of the secondary community. This may not be possible immediately, as all the students need a few weeks to settle into the new environment. But by the end of the first term many students will be ready to be treated as responsible members of the community, or at least their section of it.

- All these structural changes, however difficult they are, will be effective only if they lead to a commitment to teaching, learning and assessment strategies conducive to the improvement of students' motivation and self–efficacy. Teachers in the revitalised junior section of the school will now adopt teaching approaches designed to appeal to the interests and varied learning styles of their students. Timely and appropriate training opportunities school can help of course, but only when they truly connect with the daily realities of school life. Rather than sending teachers one at a time to day courses outside school, teams of teachers need to work together, on or off the school premises, planning new ideas, gathering resources, trying things and appropriate out, supporting and observing each others' efforts, sharing experience among themselves and with the rest of the school.

- Part of this teacher development strategy will necessarily involve making and maintaining close links with their colleagues in other schools around them in the community, from whom they draw their students. The shared agenda among this group of teachers should be much closer now, as the way they work is not so different as it may have been previously, particularly where the senior primary teachers are themselves trying out strategies to introduce their final year students to more than one or two teachers. They may still struggle with the different perceptions of teaching inherited from their personal experience and their training, but the commonalities should prevail. The logistics of working together periodically may be tricky too, but with so much to learn from each other there will be a stronger motivation to work things out with all the pragmatism we are renowned for.

- When a group of people who work in different buildings are committed to working with each other, technology can be increasingly helpful. Once teachers have met in person enough to know and trust each other, and understand a little about how each others' minds work, then the use of Email and fax, even their own web site, can make communication both easy and effective. There are costs involved in setting up the necessary communications systems, but for many schools it would mean adapting existing systems rather than creating new ones. The improvement in the quality and continuity of learning for the students could be considerable.

It will take teacher action and teacher development to change the pedagogy of teaching. From there it requires some short but significant steps to develop the fifth and last of our 'bridges of progression', involving both students and their teachers in the management of learnin

The Management–of–Learning Bridge

This is the point at which we need to return to the research studies and advice offered about the connection between formative assessment and student achievement. The key studies in this field were mentioned in Chapter Two and are fully detailed in the further reading list. In 1998, Paul Black and Dylan Wiliam published their own summary of their research in a little booklet called 'Inside the black box: Raising standards through classroom assessment'. The black box of the title is a place where no light shines, and it refers in this case to classrooms which have been chronically neglected by the bright light of research and understanding. It is the daily behaviours of teachers,· the researchers argue, which have most influence on the achievement of their students, not the major structural changes so beloved of politicians, or mandatory national testing which generates results but doesn't necessarily change anything. 'Weighing the pig doesn't make it grow' could be another sub–title for their criticism of testing as the means to school improvement.

It may sound odd to focus so much on assessment when our goal is improved learning: early on in 'Inside the black box', Black and Wiliam clarify their terms to explain the essential link between the two:

"In this paper, the term 'assessment' refers to all those activities undertaken by teachers, *and by their students in assessing themselves*, which provide information to be used as feedback to modify the teaching and learning activities in which they are engaged. *Such assessment becomes 'formative assessment' when the evidence is actually used to adapt the teaching work to meet the needs."* (page 2, the italics are the in the original)

The authors then develop their argument that formative assessment can demonstrably improve the measured performance of students, and that this therefore should be a major focus for any education system interested in improving standards. They also offer several key points gleaned from their extensive review of research findings from 1988 to 1998 about the key characteristics of effective formative assessment. Here are the key points highlighted in their booklet:

- "For formative assessment to be productive, pupils should be trained in self–assessment so that they can understand the main purposes of their learning and thereby grasp what they need to achieve."

- "Opportunities for pupils to express their understanding should be designed into any piece of teaching, for this will initiate the interaction whereby formative assessment aids learning."

- "The dialogue between pupils and teacher should be thoughtful, reflective, focused to evoke and explore understanding, and conducted so that all pupils have an opportunity to think and to express their ideas."

- "Tests and homework exercises can be an invaluable guide to learning, but the exercises must be clear and relevant to learning aims. The feedback on them should give each pupil guidance on how to improve, and each must be given opportunity and help to work at the improvement."

These messages are not new to teachers. They are the fundamentals of good teaching and assessment practice, whatever the age of the students. To achieve them consistently in our schools is not easy, especially with current distractions and the flurry of external change. We may need to teach less in order for the students to learn more. Teach less, more carefully, and discuss it more with our students. We need to clarify the the purpose and expected outcomes of the tasks we design for students, and give then specific, clear and constructive feedback, and the chance to use that feedback to improve their own work. Self–correction, not just self–assessment, is the key strategy for students, for which they will need coaching and encouragement, and to be convinced that this is really adult stuff.

The Black and Wiliam study was followed up by a further group of UK researchers who call themselves the Assessment Reform Group. Their contribution to our understanding was published in 1999, under the title of 'Assessment for Learning: Beyond the black box', which could be a very confusing title for someone who had missed the link with the earlier booklet.

This new booklet fleshed out the strategies which follow from an acceptance of the importance of formative assessment in learning improvement. Several characteristics of assessment for improved learning were described, each of which has implications for what teachers and schools – both primary and secondary – need to do.

"The characteristics of assessment that promotes learning are that:

- it is embedded in a view of teaching and learning of which it is an essential part;

- it involves sharing learning goals with pupils;

- it aims to help pupils to know and to recognise the standards they are aiming for;

- it involves pupils in self–assessment;

- it provides feedback which leads to pupils recognising their next steps and how to take them;

- it is underpinned by the confidence that every pupil can improve;

- it involves both pupils and teachers reviewing and reflecting on assessment data."

Even while the researchers are finding out about the things that really work and synthesising them for us in this way, teachers in classrooms are developing strategies like this:

Coaching the Skill of Self–Correction to Improve Students' Learning

Step One

The teaching resource is a piece of student work, probably produced by a student in the previous year, completed to meet certain outcomes and assessment criteria. Keep both the chosen piece and the criteria quite simple at this stage. Make and distribute a copy of the piece of work (without the original student's name of course) to every student in the group, and explain the outcomes and the criteria it was trying to meet. Now take the students through it as a teacher–directed exercise, explaining how you would 'mark' and comment on the work, with respect to the given criteria.

You might try this from time to time with the students, just to model the process for them and let them see how it's done. The teacher is thinking aloud for the students, to let them into the secret garden of how judgements of the quality of their work are made.

Step Two

When you think most or at least a fair proportion of your students are ready, divide the group into 'mixed–ability' sub–groups of four or five, so there are two or three students in each group who are clear what to do. Give each group copies of a piece of student work along with a written copy of the outcomes and criteria it is based on. The criteria will be the same for each group, but they will each have a different piece of work to look at. The group's task, working together and thinking aloud, is to 'mark' and comment on the piece of work, with reference to the criteria. They have to be able to justify the judgements they are making, and record both the judgements and their reasons on a piece of paper. Also on the sheet, the group will write down the feedback they would give to the student who did the work, about what has been done and the suggested steps to improve. Then the work and the comments and feedback sheet are passes on to another group.

Each group reviews the piece it has received from the previous group. They look at the judgements and comments and decide whether they agree, or the reasons for disagreement. Then they look at the feedback. Was it intelligible, constructive and helpful? How could the feedback have been improved, if at all?

The teacher then asks for a report from each group about what they have seen and concluded. Together they review the importance of the criteria in determining judgement, and the characteristics of useful feedback.

This step, like Step One, could be repeated several time while the students learn and practice how to assess well and provide good feedback.

Step Three

When the teacher thinks that most of the students are ready to have a go on their own, s/he selects another piece of student work and distributes it, together with the criteria to guide the assessment. This time students do the exercise on their own, before sharing what they've done with a partner. As with any learning task, when the students are at different stages of 'readiness', the teacher may personally support some students, put them with a learning partner, or use an easier piece with fewer criteria, matching the task to the needs of the student. If a student is developing the skill more rapidly, or to a higher level of sophistication, the teacher provides a more challenging task.

Many teachers recognise this exercise as almost identical to the process of 'moderating' used in the assessment of students' work for public examinations. *Like their teachers, students need the chance to learn how to apply criteria accurately and confidently as part of learning to self–assess and self–correct. If they are to be involved in peer assessment, they must first learn how to separate feedback about the task from feedback about the person.*

Of course, teaching and assessing to pre–set criteria would constitute one approach to teaching, and not be used all the time. If it were, we would train students as good 'recipe–followers' rather than good learners, and restrict their thinking to convergent rather than divergent tracks. Some activities will present a stimulus and encourage students to respond, without the certainty of a 'right' answer. If certain outcomes are expected, it is very empowering for students to have them clarified and modelled in this way, rather than just explained in the abstract.

Self–correction is an essential part of being an autonomous learner, which all education systems have as a goal for their students.

The Link with Records of Achievement

Some teachers reading this will recognise the processes of review and student involvement as a familiar part of the process of 'Records of Achievement' which continues to flourish in many schools.

Such records, and the processes which underpin them, are one way of addressing the 'management–of–learning' bridge between schools. Before the students move on, they reflect on their most recent learning and development, find and review the evidence of such learning within school and beyond, and include it in their 'portfolio' of selected interesting items. A small further selection from among these items might be offered to the next school, to illuminate important aspects of the student's learning which would be of interest to their new teachers.

Jim Whittaker's cartoon shows what some primary school teachers suspect happens to those records as they are offered by the incoming students. As with all the cartoons, an idea is extrapolated to the absurd, to make the point and to make us laugh, and to remind us of the fish–hooks in the mass of attitudes and practice we are trying to disentangle.

If the secondary school is genuinely interested in the prior learning of the student, as part of their pursuit of properly differentiated learning, then the Records of Achievement will be looked at carefully, even if they are then returned to the student. One item within the record, perhaps the letter written by the

student about themselves, could be made more widely available to the new teachers. An example of the student's unaided writing in the term before transfer might also prove useful to everyone. So might a piece of work considered by the student's last teacher to be the best they had produced in the previous term, to use as a benchmark for quality in the first shaky few weeks. Teachers find it very useful to know exactly what the student can do as they adjust their expectations. The research on gender and attainment has suggested that boys especially may produce for their teachers what they think their teachers will accept, and no more. The transition into a new school, or even into a new classroom, could lead to a small but significant drop in expectation and effort unless the teacher is alerted to the standards which are within the student's extended grasp.

The contents of a Record of Achievement will always have a limited 'shelf–life'. They represent a contemporary snapshot of the student, and can never reflect either the entirety of the person nor the dynamic aspects of their development. Useful and interesting though the contents may be – and they certainly deserve better treatment than the shredder – it's the process which generated the items which is more lasting and important. This where students begin to reflect on and take more responsibility for their own learning and development. Only learners can improve their learning: the job of teachers and schools is to encourage them to do so, and to provide the structures and practice they need.

The habit of periodic review, self–correction, goal–setting and monitoring those goals is started in many primary schools at a very early age. It becomes part of the way students and teachers work together. Towards the end of their primary school careers, the students begin to focus on their goals for achievement in the next school, both short–term and long–term. As they enter the new school these goals come with them. They are shared with the person most closely responsible for monitoring their progress, the form tutor, and become the first items in the process of review and goal–setting which continues uninterrupted into the secondary school.

The role of the form tutor

The management–of–learning bridge is central to the development of motivation and self–efficacy from one environment to the next. The role of the form tutor is also crucial, and here again teachers will need the time, the training and the recognition to fulfil this role successfully.

Traditionally, the role of form tutor was not highly regarded by either schools or teachers. It was concerned primarily with checking attendance, overseeing the collection of homework, writing a little summary on the report and interceding occasionally with disciplinary matters. In the arcane distinctions of the school, it was a 'pastoral' role first and foremost. In many secondary schools, this has already changed, and a review of the role in the junior years at least is another useful part of improving learning continuity during those vital years when learning habits and self–efficacy are challenged by major environmental changes. Wherever possible, the form tutor should be scheduled to teach his or her own group, to increase the contact and understanding between them.

One big question

Why do you think some students resist being involved in the assessment process, and what can you do it about it?

Conclusion

Foundations of Learning Progression

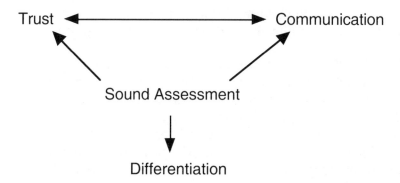

Trust ⟵————————⟶ Communication

Sound Assessment

Differentiation

From the voices of the students and the teachers, as well as the researchers, we have seen the importance of developing trust and effective liaison between the teachers as well as the managers in our various schools and stages. Trust can be built through contact and communication, but until a modicum is assured, the communication may be difficult and fraught with misunderstandings and even resentment.

Communication, in person as well as on paper or electronic, can be time–consuming and frustrating: it's not easy to find agreement on the details as well as the broad principles. Governments can cut the Gordian knot by simply mandating a uniform transition record to be used by all schools, but such central directives rarely have the impact they intended. The communication needed here is not just about the students and their needs and achievement: to cross the pedagogy bridge, teachers need to communicate with each other, across the barriers of our training and our institutional habits. Within secondary schools there is an urgent need for greater communication, also, to focus teachers on the learning of the students they share, beyond the subject loyalties which have been our main reference point for so long.

Sound assessment implies a wealth of understanding about the purpose, strategies and usefulness of assessment. It means that the information we gather about students' learning must be as accurate, consistent and fair as we can manage. It also means that the receivers of the information are both willing and able to use it when planning effective teaching for the incoming students.

And finally differentiation, a clumsy word with infinite implications for the mainstream teacher. It implies that we aim to provide teaching tailored to the individual needs of individual children, in all areas of their learning. The challenge to the primary teacher is to keep all the learning plates spinning simultaneously for all the children, balancing Science with Music and Technology and everything else, while still emphasising the basics of Numeracy and Literacy. In the secondary school most teachers see upwards of one hundred children every week, and for some teachers it is many more. Their challenge is to treat each of these children as a unique learner, whose individual needs can and should be catered for. For most teachers, absolute differentiation is an impossible goal. All we can do is strive a little closer to it each year, and cope with the continuing feeling of dissatisfaction and frustration.

Building the 'management–of–learning' bridge, and then using it to cross the divide between us, is one of the hardest and most satisfying aspects of teaching. But even now, for some teachers and students and their parents, sharing criteria with students sounds like cheating, and all the strategies for student involvement, self–correction, goal–setting, and so on are just a trendy way for teachers to avoid their professional responsibilities.

The barriers of school design, exam pressures, students' insecurities and mixed parental expectation are hard to shift.

Making Plans, Taking Action and Checking the Impact

Only you can decide how much of a priority the issue of transition is for you. You may have already gathered evidence which convinces you that too many of your students are struggling during their first year in your school. Or you may want to make use of the optional tests which the government is so thoughtfully making available for you, to confirm the situation in your school.

Having decided the extent of the concern, you have to weigh this issue against the other priorities you have already agreed and built into your school development plan. Improving students' learning, at whatever stage in your school, can never be seen as an 'initiative' as it is a continuing core purpose of yours and every other school. You may be able to weave the strands of the issue into existing priorities rather than treat this is something new and free–standing. Or you may decide that it will have to wait a while, and spend the intervening time gradually preparing the ground for the new seeds you will sow in a year or two. As we have seen throughout this book, attitudes are a critical underpinning factor, and attitudes are the slowest to change. It's never too early to think and talk before the detailed plans are laid.

The complexity of the issue demands a carefully thought through plan, keeping the various necessary factors – Trust, Communication, Sound Assessment, Differentiation – cooking simultaneously and fostering the connection between them.

As you plan, consider too how you are going to check whether the action you take turns out successfully. This means planning in your evaluation strategy from the beginning, not trying to tack it on the end as an after–thought. You may want to survey a sample of your first year students before you make any changes at all, to provide a benchmark for the degree of change your actions engender.

Monitoring often takes some time and resources which will need to be factored into your budget, and possibly into your Professional Development plans.

My hope, finally, is that my studious avoidance of 'sure–fire tips for teachers' does not put you off: our greatest resource as teachers is our deep understanding of the unique conditions in our schools and classrooms, and a large amount of common sense. These are best harnessed when we work in teams, whose combined experience and sheer brain power could move mountains. If we really want the learning continuity of all students to improve as they move into secondary school, and make it a priority for a while, then a careful selection of the strategies presented here could make a definite and positive difference. Go for it.

Further reading

All the sources below are relevant to transition from school to school.

Anderman, E.M. and Maehr, M.L. (1994) **Motivation and schooling in the middle grades** Review of Educational Research, 64, 2, 287-309

Flutter J., Rudduck J., Addams H., Johnson M., and Maden M. (1999) **Improving Learning: the Pupils' Agenda** Cambridge, Homerton Research Unit

Galton M., Gray J. and Rudduck J. (1999) **The Impact of School Transition and Transfer on Pupils' Attitudes to Learning and their Progress** London, Department for Education and Employment, Research Report RR 131

Hargreaves, L. and Galton, M. (1999) (eds.) **Moving From the Primary Classroom: Twenty Years On** London, Routledge

Hawk, K. and Hill, J. (1997) **Making Achievement Cool** Wellington, New Zealand Ministry of Education

Lee B., Harris S. and Dickson P. (1995) **Continuity and Progression 5-16: Developments in School** Slough, NFER

Nichols G. and Gardner J. (1999) **Moving between Key Stages** London, Routledge

QCA (1997) **Building bridges** London, Qualifications and Curriculum Authority

Rudduck J., Chaplain R. and Wallace G. (eds) (1996) **School Improvement: What can Pupils tell Us?** London, David Fulton

SCAA (1996) **Promoting Continuity between Key Stage 2 and Key Stage 3** Middlesex: School Curriculum and Assessment Authority

Suffolk LEA (1997) **A Report on an Investigation Into What Happens When Pupils Transfer into Their Next School at the Ages of 9, 11 and 13** Ipswich, Inspection and Advice Division, Suffolk Education Department

Wigfield, A., Eccles, J., MacIver, D., Reuman, D. and Midgley, C. (1991) **Transitions during early adolescence,** Developmental Psychology 27,4,552-565

All the following sources present research outcomes on improving the quality of teaching and learning through formative assessment

Assessment Reform Group (1999) **Assessment for Learning** University of Cambridge School of Education.

Black,P. and Wiliam,D. (1998) Assessment and **Classroom Learning** Assessment in Education 5(1), pp 7 - 74

Black,P. and Wiliam, D. (1998) **Inside the Black Box** King's College, London

Crooks, T.J. (1988) **The impact of classroom evaluation practices on students** Review of Educational Research 58, pp 438 - 481

All the following are mine, concerned with teacher development, schools' assessment practice, progression and differentiation

Sutton, R. (1995) **Assessment for Learning** Salford, RS Publications

Sutton, R. (1997) **The Learning School** Salford, RS Publications

Sutton, R. (1999) **School Quality Matters** Salford, RS Publications